Contents

Introduction

This resource is designed to help guide you through your Edexcel GCSE Music course. It contains all the information you need to succeed in your listening exam and gives guidance on how you can best approach your coursework tasks. It covers the requirements of the revised specification as published by Edexcel (for first examination in 2008). It is not designed as a replacement for your teacher, but will supplement everything your teacher tells you and also give you some ideas for your compositions.

The full set of resources consists of a student book (this book), a set of two CDs and a teacher's resource file.

The student book contains information on all the topics to be studied for Edexcel GCSE Music with performing, composing and listening tasks included. To attempt the listening tasks you will need access to the CDs containing the majority of the extracts referred to in this book. Beside each listening task is a CD and track reference, guiding you to the appropriate extract on the CDs. The student book also contains a section on understanding music, guiding you through the foundations of your musical understanding, and information on how best to approach your coursework, giving you a glimpse into what moderators are looking for in your coursework.

The teacher's resource file contains extension and foundation composition tasks and understanding music worksheets. It also contains extra information for your teacher on different aspects of teaching the course. If you feel that the composition tasks given in this book are too hard or too easy, then you should ask your teacher to photocopy the alternative tasks for you.

The student book follows the structure of the Edexcel GCSE Music specification with all the topics arranged into the Areas of Study (AoS). Each AoS has an introduction section followed by three chapters – one for each topic in the AoS. Each chapter presents you with carefully chosen listening examples for the topic plus some tasks to test your understanding of the music and your listening skills. Technical terms and musical vocabulary are highlighted in bold and defined in the glossary.

Some composing and performing tasks are included (depending on the topic), designed to extend your understanding of the concepts and to offer you opportunities to fulfil the requirements for the coursework element of the GCSE. It is recommended that you undertake all the tasks in each chapter in the order in which they appear; some later tasks may depend on you having successfully completed the earlier ones.

There are various icons used throughout the book, which signify the following.

CD1: 24 This signifies a track on the CDs showing both the CD and track number.

This signifies a listening task.

This signifies a composing task.

This signifies a performing task.

You do not need to follow the book through from start to finish, but can choose the order in which you attempt each Area of Study (AoS). However, it is recommended that you read the 'Understanding music' chapter first as this chapter will help you to understand the language used throughout the book, making sure that you have enough theoretical knowledge to get the most from your course. If you feel you need extra practice, you should ask your teacher to give you some of the worksheets from the teacher's resource file.

No musical style has just appeared out of the blue without any influences or period of development, so each chapter includes a section outlining the origins of the musical style (and sometimes its influence on other music, where relevant). It is important that you understand the context of the musical styles as questions always come up in the exam about the origins and influences of the different topics.

The chapter entitled 'Preparing your coursework' gives you information on what the moderators are looking for in composition and performance coursework. In this chapter there is much useful advice on how to attempt your compositions and performances, listing all the major pitfalls to avoid. You should read this chapter before you start any work you think might be submitted as coursework for your GCSE.

The Edexcel GCSE Music course exposes you to many styles of music from different cultures and times. Approach each topic with an open mind, trying to understand what makes the music valuable in its own right. This way you will get the most out of the course and it will expand your own musical horizons.

Area of Study 1:
Structure in Western Classical music 1600–1899

This Area of Study explores music composed over a period of just under three hundred years. During this time, there were many developments in music, including the invention and evolution of the instruments and also the formation of standard musical ensembles such as the orchestra, string quartet and so on.

Large-scale musical structures, such as the orchestral symphony, the sonata for a solo instrument, the concerto for a soloist and orchestra, the string quartet, as well as several large-scale vocal forms of opera, oratorio, and cantata all became standard.

The three topics you will study are musical forms that were used throughout this entire period as a means of organizing musical ideas into a coherent and balanced structure. They are:
- ground bass and variations
- ternary form
- rondo.

In all three cases there were two key elements present: repetition and contrast. You will examine and analyse how composers achieved both the repetition of musical material in their music, as well as being able to compose the equally important contrasting sections, achieving both variety and interest in their compositions.

Musical styles and conventions changed radically between 1600 and 1899. The three important musical periods over this time were:
- the Baroque era (c.1600–1730)
- the Classical era (c.1750–1830)
- the Romantic era (c.1800–1900).

The Baroque era

Music did not lead the way in exploring new concepts and ideas but followed innovations in the arts, literature and philosophy. Italy was the centre of culture and led the way in exploring new ideas and fashions.

The word 'baroque' is Portuguese for 'pearl' and was used in reference to the ornate architecture found in German and Italian churches of the period.

The ornate interior of St Peter's Basilica, The Vatican.

In terms of the music, there was a new emphasis on an ornamental melody part, supported by a strong bass and chords. This bass was called the *basso continuo*, performed usually by a harpsichord (or organ) playing the basic chords and a cello doubling the bass line.

The most well-known and prominent composers of this period were Johann Sebastian Bach (1685–1750), George Frideric Handel (1685–1759), Henry Purcell (c.1659–95) and Antonio Vivaldi (1678–1741).

The Classical era

The Classical era reacted against the highly ornate architecture, art and music of the Baroque era. Classical architecture and art was more concerned with grace and simplicity, and sought inspiration from the ancient world of the Greeks and Romans.

The music echoed architecture in that it had a clear-cut and balanced structure, and also a simple clarity of line – that is, an emphasis on a well-constructed and balanced melody. This interest in form and order led to the establishment of some familiar musical structures in which the ideas of symmetry and balance are found, such as symphony, concerto, sonata and string quartet.

The Parthenon on the Acropolis in Athens was one particular source of inspiration.

All composers wrote pieces for a wide variety of instruments in all three of the topics that you will study. Writing variations on well-known melodies was extremely popular, as were pieces in ternary form (including the 'minuet and trio', which often featured as the third movement in a symphony). The Classical rondo was popular, often used as an exuberant last movement in a solo concerto. During this period, the orchestra also became established.

The two most famous (and prolific) composers were Wolfgang Amadeus Mozart (1756–91) and Franz Joseph Haydn (1732–1809). Ludwig van Beethoven (1770–1827) was unusual, as he spanned two musical periods. His early music was in the Classical style, but the music written around the turn of the nineteenth century onwards was Romantic in spirit, so he is known as a Classic–Romantic.

The Romantic era

The nineteenth century was the age of Romanticism. Music was influenced by literature and painting. Writers and artists began to express ordinary human emotions and feelings about love, death, happiness, sorrow and the beauty of nature. J.M.W. Turner painted landscapes that depicted the beauty as well as the ruggedness of the natural world. Lord Byron, William Wordsworth and Percy Bysshe Shelley compared human emotions and feelings with scenes from nature in their writing.

Composers followed suit. Beethoven's *Symphony No. 6* (the *Pastoral Symphony*, first performed 1808) describes a particular scene from nature in each movement. Composers wrote expressive music that responded to a wide range of emotions. The orchestra also evolved and grew radically in size to allow for a greater dynamic range. During this period, the musical forms of variations, ternary and rondo were still popular and many famous works were composed.

Ground bass and variations

In this topic you will learn about:

- the variation form of the popular Baroque ground bass
- how variations are composed over a repeating bass part
- the role and function of the *basso continuo*
- different melodic variation techniques in the Classical era
- the idea of developing motifs from themes in Romantic variation compositions.

This topic looks at one of the most popular and oldest of musical structures in which an original theme is developed through a series of variations. This can be called **ground bass**, **theme and variations**, **chaconne** or **passacaglia**.

This form was popular in the Renaissance period with keyboard composers who composed a whole series of works to display their technical prowess on the keyboard. Often these pieces were based on well-known themes such as slow dance folk melodies or popular tunes. English composers such as William Byrd (c.1543–c.1623), John Bull (c.1562–1628), Orlando Gibbons (1583–1625) and Giles Farnaby (c.1563–1640) were known as the School of English Virginalist Composers. The **virginal** was a plucked keyboard instrument, although composers wrote pieces for all types of plucked string instruments, including the spinet and harpsichord.

The themes were often short and simple in regular four-bar phrases. This was followed by a set of variations. The variations preserved several features from the original theme such as the same phrases, harmony and cadences. Some of the techniques used in these early works are covered in this topic, for example:

- the variations progress in difficulty and complexity
- each variation concentrates on *one* particular keyboard technique or figuration
- the last variation is often a grand re-statement of the theme but with more elaborate harmony.

The English composers influenced variation writing in the early years of the 1600s. This was exploited in the popular Baroque form of the ground bass.

Glossary

chaconne and passacaglia both of these forms are alike and consist of a set of continuous variations based on a ground bass. Unlike ground bass form itself, the ground can appear in different parts of the musical texture

ground bass a Baroque form in which a bass melody called the 'ground' is played continuously to a set of variations in the other instrumental or vocal parts

theme and variations musical form featuring a theme followed by a set of variations on the theme

virginal small plucked keyboard instrument like a spinet

Baroque variations: ground bass

The ground bass, also known as the ***basso ostinato***, was used quite extensively in both instrumental and vocal music of the Baroque period. This is a composition that is a series of variations over a repeating pattern of bass notes. The music explored a variety of musical textures and became more complex as it progressed. It is called the 'ground' as this part was the lowest in the musical texture. The bass would repeat every one, two, four or eight bars. It would comprise some or all of the following elements:

- key – often a **minor** key
- notes – mainly notes of long value (crotchets and minims)
- **tempo** – slow and stately
- direction – quite often descending from **tonic** to **dominant** and **cadence** back to tonic
- mood – a solemn mood or 'lament' is common in many vocal arias
- character of bass – a serious or tragic mood can be created by using chromatic notes (**semitones**). A lighter mood can be created by the use of **diatonic** intervals.

The most common representation of the 'lament' was the four-note descending bass part, such as:

The following examples are of some famous ground basses. Notice how the first example, Dido's 'lament', essentially has this four-note descending bass with extra chromatic notes that add to the serious mood.

Dido's 'lament', Purcell

Canon in D, Pachelbel

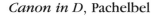

'Crucifixus' from *B minor mass*, Bach

Many of the elements outlined above are present in the examples by Purcell, Pachelbel and Bach.

Glossary

basso ostinato repeated bass melody, usually of between two to four bars duration

cadence two chords at the end of a musical phase

diatonic notes belonging to or literally 'of the key'. In diatonic harmony, these are chords in the key of the music

dominant the fifth note of the scale or key - the strongest note after the tonic

minor western tonal music in solemn sounding keys. A minor key has three semitones between the first and third notes (C-Eb)

semitone half a tone

tempo the speed of the music

tonic the first degree of a scale, the keynote

The repeating ground bass part was played continuously throughout the composition and was known as the *basso continuo* (continuous bass). It was an important element in Baroque music and was usually played by the cello and the harpsichord (organ).

The cello would play the ground bass notes and the harpsichord would play the bass with accompanying chords. The composer would indicate which chords to play with figures that represented the chords in a form of musical shorthand. This was known as **figured bass**.

Construction of variations

In general, a ground bass piece will start with just the ground played by the *basso continuo*. On the repetition of the bass, other parts are brought in and the musical texture is built up.

To achieve interest and variety, the composer will vary the number of parts playing, the type of note values used in a variation (for example quavers, semiquavers, dotted rhythms and so on), the dynamic levels, variation in **pitch** and so on.

In many pieces, the note values become shorter as the piece progresses, giving the impression of heightened drama and a sense of the music becoming faster (although the actual beat remains the same).

These features can be heard and seen in the track you will listen to in Task 1, *Canon in D* by Johann Pachelbel (1653–1706). This was originally written for three stringed instruments and bass part. The most common arrangement today is for string orchestra and that is the version you will hear. In Task 2 you will get the opportunity to compose your own ground bass.

Glossary

basso continuo literally 'a continuous bass part', usually figured to show the chords to be played by the keyboard player (harpsichord or organ). The bass line would be played by the cello (or bassoon)

figured bass numbered bass part. The figures indicate the chords to be played by the keyboard player

pitch how high or low a note(s) sounds

1 *Canon in D*, Pachelbel

Canon in D (1686) by Pachelbel has the ground bass (see the extract on page 9), which you will hear at the outset played by the cello and harpsichord.

a)   Which *three* of the following words or phrases are true of this bass part?

  i)   Equal note values   v)   All notes are played staccato
  ii) Fast   vi) Slow
  iii) Stepwise movement   vii) All leaps
  iv) Some leaps and some stepwise movement viii) Dotted notes

b)   What is the tonality of the ground bass?

  i)   Minor   iii) Modal
  ii) Major   iv) Atonal

c)   Listen to how the first part of the piece is built up and how the variations differ from each other. The first half unfolds as follows.

  * The first violin enters, playing a simple descending and ascending crotchet pattern.

Crotchets

  * Two bars later, the second violin comes in, adding another layer to the musical texture, playing crotchets in thirds to violin I.

Crotchets in thirds

  * Next there are two variations in quaver notes. This gives a sense of development and variety to the musical texture.

Quavers

  * There is further progression with two fast semiquaver variations. The music consists of scalic passages. There is a real sense of development and forward drive in the music.

Semiquavers

  * Two stately variations follow, characterized by longer note values leading to some fast demisemiquaver patterns, featuring repeated half-bar patterns called sequences.

Demisemiquavers

2 The ground bass

If you take the original Pachelbel's *Canon in D* bass and transpose it down a tone to C major, you have the following bass line.

Above the bass are the simple chords of C, F and G that will harmonize with the bass.

a) Compose your own ground bass of eight equal crotchets like Pachelbel's *Canon in D* bass, but do not use the same notes. Write your bass in C major and make sure that you start on C and end on G.

b) Using the chords written out in *Canon in D* above, add the appropriate ones to each of your own bass notes.

c) Compose *three* short variations in:

   i) crotchets

   ii) quavers

   iii) semiquavers.

Only use notes from the chords in your music. Here is a short example to help you.

Vocal music

During the Baroque era, many vocal pieces were written in ground bass form. Purcell wrote several fine examples in his famous opera called *Dido and Aeneas* (c.1689). This work was written for a girls' boarding school in Chelsea. It was based on the Classical story from Virgil's *Aeneid*. The story in brief is:

Dido, Queen of Carthage, declares her love for Aeneas, who is a Trojan prince and has just escaped from the fall of Troy. They marry, but the next day he is summoned to return to Italy to found the new Troy, which is to be called Rome. He must leave Dido behind. The opera ends with Dido, who is grief-stricken, looking forward to her own death. Her feelings are summed up in the famous ground bass lament 'When I am laid in earth'. The opera ends tragically with Dido's death.

The opera contains a series of choruses, dances and solo songs, several of which are in ground bass form.

'Farewell to Dido in Carthage' by Claude Lorrain.

3 'Ah, Belinda', *Dido and Aeneas*, Purcell

CD1: 2

'Ah, Belinda' is an aria sung by Dido near the beginning of *Dido and Aeneas* (c. 1689). The ground bass appears in straight crotchets and lasts for four bars.

Dido expresses her sorrow through the use of musical **word painting**. Here are some examples to listen out for.

Glossary

word painting
describing words in musical terms. For example 'rising' would be set to a series of ascending notes or 'grief' by falling phrases

- Long expressive minims on 'Ah'.

- Falling phrases, suggesting 'sighing'.

- Dramatic dotted and reverse dotted (lombardic) rhythms on 'prest with torment'.

- Long melismas (several notes per one word or syllable) and chromatic notes on 'torment', 'grief' and 'languish'.

- Clashing harmonies between the vocal part and bass.

- Slow tempo.
- Minor key.

Purcell makes the music appear seamless by the vocal phrases constantly overlapping with the end of the ground bass part so that continuous movement of the music is maintained. Only at the very end does the singer's phrase and bass part coincide.

4 'When I am laid in earth', *Dido and Aeneas*, Purcell CD1: 3

This is probably the most famous of all ground bass arias and has many features in common with 'Ah, Belinda'. The ground bass is printed below and you will hear this played on its own at the beginning of the extract.

a) Complete the four missing notes from the ground bass.
b) Name *three* musical features in the ground bass that help to express the feelings of sorrow in this piece.
c) What is the *basso continuo* and which two instruments play this part?
d) Which other instruments can you hear playing in this piece?
e) Which word describes the voice part?

   i) Tenor   iii) Baritone   v) Bass
   ii) Alto   iv) Soprano

f) How many times is the ground bass repeated in the extract?
g) How does the singer convey the feelings of sorrow and grief in this extract?

Chaconne and passacaglia

The only significant difference between these forms and the ground bass is that the latter might have been used less rigidly in the composition. For example, in Bach's famous *Passacaglia in C minor* for organ (1717), the ground bass moves up through the musical texture, at times in inner parts and occasionally as the top line.

Classical variations

In the Classical era composers were interested in writing pieces that explored melodic variation based on a theme heard at the start of the piece. The theme was often a familiar or popular melody. Mozart wrote several sets of variations for piano, the most famous being the twelve variations on the French folk melody 'Ah, dirai-je vous, maman?' which we know as 'Twinkle, twinkle little star'.

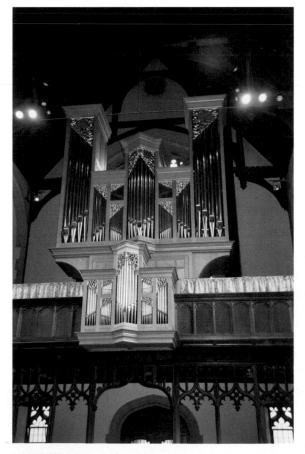

Frobenius organ in Oundle School chapel.

The usual practice was to compose several variations to start with that stuck quite closely to the theme and then gradually to become more adventurous and complex, with more subtle references to the original melody. When writing variations, the challenge for the composer was to see how much new material and invention he could extract from the original theme.

Some of the common techniques composers used to vary their themes are described in the table that follows.

Table of common variation techniques	
Melody	
Decoration	The melody can be decorated using extra notes and ornaments such as the mordent, turn, appoggiatura, acciaccatura and trill.
Counter-melody	The addition of a newly composed melody above or below the theme.
Changing position	The melody can be moved to the bass or middle part to disguise the tune.
Inversion	Turn the notes upside down (for example, G-A-B becomes B-A-G).
Augmentation	Double the note values to sound slower (for example, crotchets become minims).
Diminution	Halve the note values to sound faster (for example, crotchets become quavers).
Imitation/canon	Either free imitation of the theme in two or more parts, or a strict canon, for example 'London's burning'.
Rhythm/tempo	
Adopting a new rhythmic configuration	Using a particular rhythm pattern to disguise the theme. This could be simple flowing quavers, triplets, semiquavers, demisemiquavers, dotted (or reverse dotted) rhythms, or even a combination of several rhythms.
Change of tempo	A whole range from very slow to very fast.
Change of metre	A new time signature. For example, a piece in simple time, such as $\frac{4}{4}$, could have a variation in $\frac{3}{4}$ or $\frac{6}{8}$.
Harmony	
Different harmony	Add new harmonies to change the sound of the theme.
Change of key or mode	A variation can be in a new related key such as the dominant, subdominant, relative major/minor and so on. Quite often the tonic minor/major is used.
Instrumentation	
Change of instruments	In orchestral or ensemble pieces, a change in the instrumentation is a common variation technique.
Dynamics/articulation	
Change in articulation	For example, a legato variation might be followed by a staccato variation.

5 'Les hommes pieusement', K455, Mozart

CD1: 4

In this task you will listen to a set of ten piano variations by Mozart to discover which techniques he used to construct his variations. The variations are based on a folk melody popular at that time called 'Les hommes pieusement' (1784). Listen to the theme several times to become familiar with the melody. The outline is printed below.

Notice that:

- the theme is made up of twelve bars in a **ternary (ABA)** structure
- the middle four bars provide contrast with a new tune, a brief modulation to A minor and contrasting dynamics *f–p*, *f–p* (loud to soft, loud to soft)
- the repeat of A is *f* compared to the first four bars which are *p*. The melody is also one octave higher.

> **Glossary**
>
> **ternary (ABA)** a three part form. The first and last sections are identical or similar. The middle section (B) provides a contrast

Now you need to see how the following ten variations are constructed. Many of the techniques Mozart used are included in the table of variation techniques on page 16.

Variation 1

The theme is disguised in semiquaver figuration in the right hand. There are different dynamics from the original theme.

Variation 2

The right hand has the melody decorated with ornaments. The semiquaver figuration is now in the left-hand part.

Variation 3

There is triplet figuration in the right hand, with outline of theme in the left hand. There is also the addition of accented chromatic passing notes in the middle section.

Variation 4

This is a (loud) variation. The phrases of the theme are in octaves in the left hand, interspersed with dramatic descending semiquaver patterns in the right-hand part.

Variation 5

This is a contrasting *p* (soft) variation. It is in the tonic minor key (G minor), featuring dotted notes, triplets and semiquaver rhythms, and chromatic parts in bass and treble. Listen out for the theme in the bass in the central four-bar section.

Variation 6

The theme in two-part chords moves from left to right hand. Long trills sounding as tonic (G) and dominant (D) pedals accompany the melody. Again, this variation becomes chromatic towards the end.

Variation 7

Piano (soft) dynamic throughout. A largely four-part homophonic rendering (a). Imitation and sequences (c) are heard between the hand parts (b). Again, there are many chromatic notes.

Variation 8

By contrast to variation 7, this is *forte* (loud) throughout. The outline of the theme is in left-hand octaves, with some left-hand crossing over right-hand part. This is elaborate virtuoso display! There is also a simple semiquaver accompaniment figure in the middle of the texture. The variation breaks up towards the end into a cadenza-like section.

Variation 9

After the drama of the previous variation, there follows an 'Adagio' variation. This is a lengthy section of some 48 bars. It is dominated by a right-hand melody, which is highly ornate, wide ranging and uses many different rhythm patterns. There are quasi '*fantasia*' sections, exploiting ascending and descending chromatic scale passages.

Variation 10

Marked 'Allegro'. Change of metre to triple time $\frac{3}{8}$. Dance like, 'one-in-a-bar' feel. The piece ends with a dramatic diminished seventh chord, resolving onto a $\frac{6}{4}$ chord of G major. This leads into a short cadenza before the $\frac{3}{8}$ section returns. Another trilled dominant seventh chord (D7) takes the variation directly into the return of the theme.

Final statement of theme

It was quite common to have a final statement of the theme to conclude the variations. The repeated G, heard in the left hand throughout the middle of the movement is a 'tonic pedal'. Following the final scalic ascent, the work ends with a strong G major chord.

Romantic variations

In the Romantic era, the composition of pieces in variation form continued to flourish. Writing variations that developed **motifs** (or fragments) from the original theme became more popular than just writing melodic variations.

Johannes Brahms (1833–97) adopted this compositional technique in his sets of variations. In *Variations on a Theme of Haydn* (1873), Brahms takes a theme by Haydn that comes from a **divertimento** for wind instruments known as the *Chorale St Antoni*.

This theme had lots of interesting and unusual features for Brahms to draw upon. For example:

- unusual phrase lengths – the first section is 2 x 5 bars; the second, 4 x 4 bars, and the third section is 1 x 3 bars
- repeated notes – the nine times repeated B flats at the end
- harmony – simple diatonic B flat major
- characteristic rhythm – dotted quaver, semiquaver and then two quavers (♪♫ ♪♫).

> **Glossary**
>
> **divertimento** an 18th century suite of movements of light music for a small number of players (Italian for entertainment)
>
> **motifs** short melodic or rhythmic ideas that are used as a basis for manipulation and development in a musical composition

Eight variations follow the theme, then a finale, which is actually built on a repeated ground bass of five bars length derived from the theme (X = theme of ground bass). There are seventeen variations within this finale. It also shows how ground bass movements were still popular and used well into the nineteenth century.

6 *Variations on a Theme of Haydn*, Brahms

CD1: 5

Listen to the theme in full, followed by variations one and two.

The following questions relate to the theme.

a) What is the time signature for this extract?

   i) $\frac{2}{4}$ iii) $\frac{4}{2}$

   ii) $\frac{3}{2}$ iv) $\frac{6}{8}$

b) Name the two instrumental families that have the main melody at the start.

c) What is the tempo of this extract?

   i) Adagio   iii) Allegro

   ii) Andante   iv) Vivace

The following questions relate to the variations.

Variation 1

d) Name *one* change in the instrumentation in this variation.

e) Which feature of the original theme is developed in this variation?

   i) Dotted rhythm figure   iii) Minor key   v) Minim chords

   ii) Repeated B flats   iv) Same tempo

f) Describe what happens to the dynamics toward the end of the variation.

Variation 2

g) What is the tonality of this extract?

   i) Atonal   iii) Minor

   ii) Major   iv) Modal

h) Which aspect of the original theme is developed in this variation?

i) What do you notice about the tempo of this variation compared to the theme?

7 Variations

Brahms' 'Lullaby' (1869)

For this task you need to choose one motif (either a rhythm pattern or a few notes of melody) from the famous Brahms' 'lullaby' and then compose one variation. This will show how skilled you are at creating new musical material from just one idea. To help you with this task, the brackets on the music suggest some possible motifs.

Compose your variation specifically for your own instrument and then arrange to perform this in your lesson.

Ternary form

In this topic you will learn about:
- the essential ideas of repetition and contrast in this musical form
- the Baroque ternary structure of the 'da capo aria'
- the ternary 'minuet and trio' of the Classical era
- Romantic 'character pieces' in ternary form.

Ternary form is probably one of the most common of all musical structures and, like variation form, it goes back a long way. 'Ternary' means made up of three parts (or sections). In this case, the three parts in the musical form are commonly represented as ABA.

In this simple structure you should be able to see two important elements that are at the heart of all musical forms:
- repetition – in this case, music from section A is repeated
- contrast – which is provided by the new music of section B.

The contrasts that a composer uses in a particular piece of music will vary, of course. Some common techniques might include a new or different:
- theme
- instrumentation
- key
- metre
- rhythm
- mood
- **pitch**
- **tempo**.

In the previous chapter, you looked at examples of variations throughout the Baroque, Classical and Romantic eras. This chapter will also look at one example of a ternary form piece taken from each of these periods.

Baroque ternary – the 'da capo aria'

Composers of vocal music in the Baroque era often used ternary form to structure their music. On the music itself there are two printed sections: an A section followed by a contrasting B section. On the musical score the instruction '**da capo al fine**' would have been written at the end of the B section.

Glossary

da capo al fine instruction placed at the end of a piece meaning go back to the beginning (da capo means 'from the head') and end at the word 'fine'

pitch how high or low a note sounds

tempo the speed of the music

ternary a musical structure made up of three parts

'Da capo al fine' is Italian for 'from the beginning to the end' ('da capo' means 'from the head') and then end at the word 'fine' ('fine' means 'the end'), which appears at the end of section A. The piece was therefore in ABA ternary form.

It was the convention in the Baroque period for the singer to **improvise** ornaments and extra notes during the repeat of section A. This made it different from the first A section and also made each individual interpretation of the piece unique.

The most well known of all choral works from the Baroque era is probably the **oratorio** *Messiah* (1741–2) by Handel. An oratorio is a work that takes words and stories from the Bible and sets them to music. *Messiah* is written in three distinct sections and tells the biblical story of the birth, death and resurrection of Jesus Christ. In this large-scale work, Handel included a number of solo 'da capo arias'. One of the most well known of these is the bass solo aria 'The trumpet shall sound'.

Glossary

improvise make up music spontaneously

oratorio large scale musical setting for chorus, soloists and orchestra of a biblical text

1 'The trumpet shall sound', *Messiah*, Handel

CD1: 6

'The trumpet shall sound' is an exciting piece for the bass soloist with an important part called an **obbligato** (meaning a part that is obligatory and not optional) for trumpet. The string orchestra also provides the accompaniment to the voice and trumpet parts.

Glossary

obbligato prominent solo part in the musical texture

a) Listen to the opening of section A, which has the following words:
    'The trumpet shall sound and the dead shall be raised incorruptible.'

The mood is uplifting and positive. How is this achieved in the music?

b) Now listen to the opening of section B, which has the following words:

'For this corruptible must put on incorruption and this mortal must put on immortality.'

These words create a more serious and sober mood, which is matched by a contrast in the music to that in section A. How is this achieved in the music?

It was quite common for a da capo aria like this to express two different emotions or moods through the words. The prevailing emotion would be the words from section A as this formed two-thirds of the composition. In this case, the mood (which was called in Baroque times the **affection**) is triumphant, as mirrored in the words, 'the dead shall be raised incorruptible'.

Glossary

affection refers to the prevailing mood or emotion expressed in the music of the Baroque era

2 Black and white, chalk and cheese

In this task you need to compose two short contrasted melodies for an instrument of your own choice and then perform them to the rest of the class.

a) You could work with a partner and write one melody each. The melodies should be strongly contrasted in at least *two* ways, using the suggestions below.
   - A major key in one melody contrasted with a minor key in the other.
   - Two contrasted tempos – for example, slow/fast.
   - Mainly high notes in one melody contrasted with mainly low notes in the other.
   - Simple rhythms, for example crotchets and quavers, contrasted with dotted rhythms, triplets and so on in the other.

b) Give your composition an imaginative title that suggests contrasts such as 'The angel and the devil', 'Black and white', 'Chalk and cheese' and so on.

c) When you have completed your composition, perform your melodies to the rest of the class. With the help of your teacher, evaluate your work. Which melodies were contrasted effectively and how was this achieved? Which melodies were too similar to each other and why?

Classical ternary – the 'minuet and trio'

In the Classical era, many pieces were written in ternary form. It was ideal for short pieces as well as for longer movements. A ternary structure that also became very popular at this time was the **minuet and trio**, which was often used as the third movement in a symphony. Another popular ternary structure of this time was the **scherzo and trio**.

Originally, the minuet was a Baroque dance of moderate speed in triple time and would have been paired with a second minuet often called the trio (as it was written in just three parts and provided a good contrast to the first minuet). The practice was to repeat the first dance, so giving the ABA or ternary structure. Within each section, the music was further subdivided so that the A and B sections themselves were in ternary form. The minuet and trio survived well into the Classical era.

Like Mozart, Haydn was also a great classical composer. He composed a huge amount of music in all forms. He wrote an incredible 104 symphonies. In many of these the third movement is a minuet and trio. Many of these works had nicknames such as 'The Drum Roll', 'The Farewell', 'The Bear'. In Task 3 you are going to listen to the minuet and trio from *Symphony No. 101* (1794), called 'The Clock', mainly because of the 'tick-tock' accompaniment in the second movement.

Glossary

minuet and trio a ternary form structure, performed as minuet-trio-minuet. The minuet is a stately dance in triple time and the contrasting middle section (trio) usually features a reduction in instrumental parts

scherzo and trio a ternary (ABA) structure, in which the scherzo section is repeated. The scherzo is a lively and fast movement (scherzo is Italian for 'joke'), while the contrasting trio section has a reduced orchestration and/or number of parts

3 'Minuet and trio', *Symphony No. 101*, Haydn

CD1: 7

a) Listen several times to the minuet, followed by the trio from the third movement of *Symphony No.101* (1794) by Haydn.

The minuet

The trio

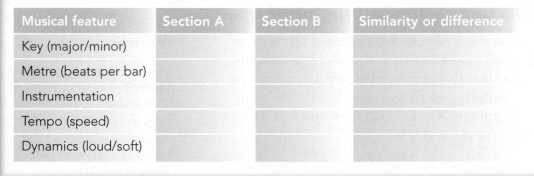

On a copy of the table below, make a list of the similarities and differences between the two sections. Be careful, as some musical elements are the same. Can you spot them?

Musical feature	Section A	Section B	Similarity or difference
Key (major/minor)			
Metre (beats per bar)			
Instrumentation			
Tempo (speed)			
Dynamics (loud/soft)			

Romantic 'character pieces' in ternary form

In the Romantic era, composers wrote ternary form pieces for both solo instruments as well as for large ensembles such as the symphony orchestra. Ternary form was probably one of the most commonly used musical structures of all time as it provided composers with the ideal way in which to achieve both repetition and contrast in a musical composition.

The Russian composer Peter Tchaikovsky (1840–93) wrote several famous ballet scores, including the enduringly popular Christmas tale of 'The Nutcracker', (1892). The story is as follows.

The scene is a party on Christmas Eve and two children, Clara and Franz, have become argumentative because they have not been allowed to leave the room with their presents: a doll and a toy soldier. To try to calm them down, Uncle Drosselmeyer gives them a nutcracker to play with, which unfortunately Franz breaks. Clara takes the nutcracker and doll and puts them both to bed. What follows is the magical adventures in Clara's dream: the toy soldiers, led by the nutcracker (who has become a handsome prince), battle with the mice and their king. Clara is transported to the land of the Snow King and Queen and is then led by the Sugar-Plum Fairy into the Kingdom of Sweets…

A scene from the ballet, The Nutcracker.

Many of the short 'character pieces' in this story are written in ternary form, and these are designed to be descriptive of a particular mood or scene.

4 'Marche', *The Nutcracker*, Tchaikovsky

CD1: 8

Listen to the 'Marche' from this suite by Tchaikovsky. It occurs at the point in the story when Franz is playing with his toy soldier. The music conjures up an exciting military scene of soldiers on the parade ground.

The following questions relate to section A.

a) Which two families of instruments play the opening four bars of the theme?
b) Which family of instruments plays the following four bars?
c) What is the time signature for this extract?
   i) 3/4   iii) 4/4
   ii) 3/2   iv) 6/8
d) How is a military mood created in the music in this section?

The following questions relate to section B.

e) How would you describe this contrasted melody in section B? Is it:
   i) a melody played by the brass instruments only in rising quavers
   ii) a woodwind melody in semiquavers, playing a rising scale pattern
   iii) a melody split between woodwind and strings in a descending semiquaver pattern?
f) What is the tonality of this section of music?
   i) Major   iii) Modal
   ii) Minor   iv) Atonal
g) What musical device can be heard in quavers throughout this B section?
   i) Riff   iii) Descant
   ii) Pedal   iv) Imitation

The following question compares the two A sections.

h) In terms of the instrumentation, mention one way in which Tchaikovsky adds variety to the repeat of section A.

Rondo

In this topic you will learn about:

- the essential ideas of repetition and contrast in this musical form
- the origins of rondo in Baroque ritornello form
- the evolution of the 'simple' rondo of the Classical era
- the popularity of rondos throughout the Classical and Romantic periods.

The word '**rondo**' comes from the French word 'rondeau', which means 'to come around'. It is a simple idea – a memorable melody keeps on coming round, in between which there are contrasting sections (called **episodes**) to provide variety. The two important features of repetition and contrast appear in the same piece.

Simple rondo form was an extension of **ternary** form (see pages 22–27):

- ternary = ABA
- simple rondo = ABACA.

Larger scale rondos could have any number of episodes: ABACADAEA and so on.

The rondo evolved from a slightly different form in the Baroque era called **ritornello** (which means 'a little return').

Baroque rondo – ritornello

The ritornello was used extensively in the first movements of Baroque **concertos** by composers such as Vivaldi and Bach. The main difference between rondo and ritornello is that in the ritornello the main theme does not always appear in the home key on each return apart from the last statement at the end of the movement.

Vivaldi is probably best known for his set of four violin concertos *The Four Seasons* (c.1725). A concerto is a piece for a solo instrument and an orchestra, and ritornello is an ideal form for contrasting the **tutti** (full) sections with the **solo** (in this case the violin). Sometimes this solo part might feature several instruments and is called the **concertante** group.

Glossary

concertante name given to the solo or solo group in a Baroque concerto grosso

concerto piece for a solo instrument or solo group of instruments and orchestra. The form has three movements, usually fast-slow-fast

episodes contrasting musical section (for example in ritornello and rondo forms)

ritornello Baroque 'rondo' form featuring alternating sections of the ritornello theme and contrasting episodes. The episodes were often solo sections in a reduced instrumental texture

rondo classical form comprising a series of rondo sections interspersed with contrasting episodes. The simple rondo was structured as ABACA, where A = the rondo theme and B and C = the episodes

solo a part for one instrument

ternary a musical structure made up of three parts

tutti Italian for 'all', meaning that everyone plays at this point in the music

1 *Violin Concerto in A minor, 1st movement*, Vivaldi CD1: 9

Vivaldi's *Violin Concerto in A minor* op 3. no. 6 (1711) is scored for the following instruments: solo violin, strings (violins I and II, viola, cello) and continuo (harpsichord).

The plan of the movement is printed below. First listen to the ritornello theme several times to get to know the music well. It lasts for twelve bars only and contains two main musical ideas that you will hear developed during the movement: the repeated note idea, labelled (a), and the arpeggio idea, labelled (b).

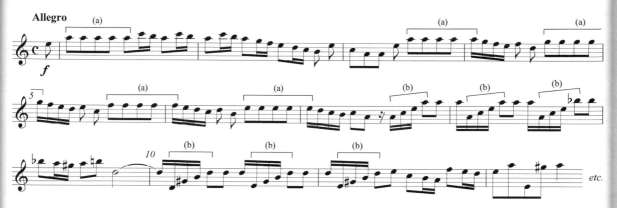

Try to follow the plan of the movement as you listen to the music.

Bars	Section	Key	Musical features
1–12	Ritornello	A minor	Complete statement of theme
12–21	Solo	A minor to C major (relative major)	Solo uses opening idea (a) of theme. The music modulates to C major
21–23	Ritornello	A minor	Brief – just three bars of the ritornello
23–35	Solo	Starts in A minor, then passes through several keys to end in E minor (dominant key of A minor)	Exciting semiquaver passage work on the solo violin
35–44	Ritornello	E minor (dominant)	Central ritornello in dominant key
44–57	Solo	Various keys, but ends in A minor	Develops idea (a) from theme
57–60	Ritornello	A minor	Start of final ritornello based on idea (a) from theme
60–68	Solo	A minor	Violin interrupts the ritornello
68–end	Ritornello	A minor	Continuation of ritornello based on idea (b) from theme

2 Roundabout ritornello

Compose your own ritornello that has no end, it just keeps on going round and round. To do this, you need to make sure that the end of your ritornello links back to the beginning.

a) Write twelve bars and choose your own key and time signature. You should write for your own instrument or voice. Remember that this needs to be catchy and memorable because in a ritornello the main tune is heard many times. Here is an example.

Ritornello theme from 'Autumn' from *The Four Seasons* by Vivaldi

b) When you have finished, perform your ritornello to each other in class.

A Classical rondo

In the Classical era, the rondo flourished and was used by composers in many types of music, from small-scale keyboard pieces to whole concerto and symphony movements.

The biggest difference between a ritornello and a rondo is the key of the theme when it returns throughout the course of the piece. With a ritornello, this would often come back in different related keys until its last statement, which would then have been in the tonic key of the movement. In a rondo, the main theme nearly always comes back in the tonic key.

In both forms, the reprise of the rondo/ritornello theme would quite often be a shortened version. If the original melody was 24 bars long, the repeat might be only eight or twelve bars long but would clearly feature the main musical ideas from the theme. The last repeat would usually be the full and complete statement of the theme.

The contrasting episode sections are often in closely related keys to the home key such as the **subdominant**, **dominant**, relative **major**/**minor** (see page 31 for glossary definitions). This provides a good contrast to the key of the rondo theme.

Painting by Heinrich Lossow showing Mozart playing the organ for the first time (painted c. 1864).

As an example of the form on a relatively miniature scale of only 62 bars, the listening piece in Task 3 is a simple rondo in F for piano by Mozart. The piece comes from the *London Notebook*, which is from a collection of keyboard pieces composed during the Mozart family's visit to London in 1764. Mozart wrote this piece when he was only eight years old!

3 *Rondo in F*, K15, Mozart   CD1: 10

The form in this piece is simple rondo ABACA. The sections are marked on the score. Notice that the final A section is the repeat of bars 1–16. The direction 'D.C. al Fine' tells you to go back to the beginning and end at 'fine' (bar 16).

Listen to the *Rondo in F* and discuss the following three questions with your teacher.

a) What do you think is the character or mood of the rondo theme and how is this achieved in the music?

b) Describe the music of the two episodes, B and C. Mention the key, mood and character of each section of music.

c) Do you think that the episodes contrast well with the rondo theme? How are these contrasts achieved in the music?

4 Rondo round the class!

The music printed below is part of the famous rondo theme (1692) by Marc-Antoine Charpentier (1643–1704). You may recognize this as the theme music to the Eurovision Song Contest!

a) Compose one 'episode' for your own instrument to help create a large-scale class rondo. Make sure that your melody contrasts to the rondo theme in at least *one* way.

b) When you have finished, perform your piece. If possible, practise the rondo theme so that as many of you as possible can play it with your teacher.

A Romantic rondo

Nineteenth-century composers also found the rondo to be a versatile musical structure. Beethoven often reverted back to the 'ritornello' idea of having the theme recur in different keys for dramatic effect, but, generally, composers did not change the form much. Occasionally an introduction was added as well as a concluding section called a **coda**. Sometimes short sections, called links, joined together an episode to the rondo theme. Georges Bizet (1838–75) used the rondo form in the **overture** to his famous opera *Carmen* (1873–4).

The story is set in Seville in Southern Spain and follows the exploits of Carmen, an attractive gypsy girl, who, at the start of the opera, is working in a cigarette factory. One day she picks a fight with a girl and injures her with a knife. Don Jose, an impressionable young corporal in the Dragoons, arrests her. She persuades him to let her go and he is then imprisoned for his own incompetence.

Carmen joins her gypsy friends in smuggling activities in the mountains and when Don Jose is released, he deserts the army and joins her. However, Carmen soon tires of him in favour of the handsome toreador Escamillo. Don Jose is intensely jealous and when Carmen just laughs at him, he lunges at her with a knife and stabs her. The opera ends in tragedy as Carmen falls dying to the ground.

An overture is the orchestral music that is played at the beginning of the performance while the curtain is still down. It is used to set the scene and give the listener a flavour of the place where the music is set, in this case Spain. The custom was to use the overture to preview some of the main tunes that the listener would hear during the course of the entire opera.

Rondo form was ideal for this overture as the two episodes, B and C, are contrasting operatic tunes from the opera. The opening bars of the rondo theme A and the two episodes, B and C, are printed on the next page to help you find your way round the piece

5 The overture from *Carmen*, Bizet

CD1: 11

Opening bars of the rondo theme

Episode B

Episode C

Now listen to the piece several times and then answer the following questions.

The following questions relate to the rondo theme.

a) How many times do you hear the opening four bars in the rondo theme?
b) What is an appropriate tempo and dynamic level for this section?
c) Which ornament is heard on the minim at the end of most four-bar phrases?

    i)   Mordent
    ii) Turn
    iii) Trill
    iv) Appoggiatura

The following questions relate to episode B.

d) Name *two* ways in which contrast to the rondo theme is achieved in the first half of this episode.

e) Which of the following is true about the music in the second half of this episode?
    i)   A legato melody played in thirds in brass and strings.
    ii) A staccato melody played in octaves in woodwind and strings.
    iii) A staccato melody played in octaves in woodwind and brass.

The following questions relate to episode C.

f) Describe the opening part of this episode by completing the following statement:
    'The accompanying staccato chords heard at the outset are played by the t_____ and the t_____. The melody itself is played in o_____ by all the s_____ family.'

g) When this melody is repeated, what differences can you detect in the instrumentation and dynamics?

h) This episode appears later in the opera and is called 'The toreador's song'. Name *one* feature of the music that makes this suitable to depict a march.

Area of Study 2:

Changing directions in Western Classical music from 1900

The twentieth century saw more technological advances than ever before, and at a greater pace than anyone might have thought possible. From the public adoption of motorcars rather than horse-drawn carriages through to the worldwide use of computers and the Internet; from the birth of air travel through to probes being sent to the far reaches of our solar system, the advances in science, medicine and technology have been unprecedented.

In music, the invention of a means to record music and broadcast it to the general public has seen a complete change in the way music is produced and distributed, and it is still changing. Music can now be downloaded from the Internet so that we can listen to and buy any music we like without having to step outside of our homes. This is a far cry from having to go to the concert hall or play the music yourself if you wanted to listen to it.

In Victorian times, going to the concert hall was one of the few opportunities to listen to music.

As the twentieth century has progressed music has become widely available.

Two World Wars, the invention of weapons that could end all life on the planet, the eradication or control of many diseases, the ability to travel from one end of the world to the other in a very short space of time and to predict the forces of nature have all contributed to great changes to the way we see the world and each other. Artists, writers and composers have been influenced by all these factors and the social changes that go with them.

The twentieth century has witnessed more developments in music than has ever been seen before. Composers reacted to what they saw as the emotionalism or indulgence of the Romantic era in different ways, leading to strikingly varied styles of composition. None of this happened overnight, and many of the ideas and compositional styles we now take for granted took many years to become accepted by the musical world, and many more years before the labels we recognize were attached to them.

The main musical styles of the twentieth century	
Impressionism	Expressionism
Serialism	Neo-classicism
Jazz-influenced music	Nationalism
Avant-garde music	Experimental music
Indeterminacy (aleatoric music)	Electronic music
Post-modernism	Minimalism

Composers did not always limit themselves to one musical style – many, such as Igor Stravinsky (1882–1971), adopted one style for a part of their composing careers and then moved on to something different when they felt they needed to express themselves in a different way. Indeed, many of the styles listed above overlap significantly and may even be combined in one piece of music.

Like most earlier eras, twentieth-century composers either embraced traditional forms and concepts, trying to take them further so as to find their own 'voice', or they went the other way, denouncing all that had gone before and experimenting with completely new concepts and compositional techniques.

In this book we will be looking at several of these musical styles. They are:

- expressionism
- minimalism
- experimental and electronic music.

We will explore what influenced the composers to write the type of music they did, what the central music concepts are behind each style, and what techniques you might adopt from these composers to write music of your own.

Expressionism and serialism

In the chapter on expressionism we will look at what influenced the development of expressionism and serialism. We will look at the work of 'The Second Viennese School' and how their achievements changed how composers of later generations viewed tonality and key relationships. We will study the techniques used in writing a serialist piece and how you might use these to write your own piece in this style.

Minimalism

La Monte Young (b.1935) was an experimental composer who was fascinated with drones and repetition. His experiments led to the development of minimalism. Later composers such as Steve Reich (b.1936) and Philip Glass (b.1937) refined the style and brought it to the attention of a wider audience. In the chapter on minimalism we will look at the way musical elements are used in a minimalist piece and how minimalist composers developed and extended their ideas.

Experimental and electronic music

Most composers experiment with new instruments as they are developed and try to establish their own creative voice by using accepted compositional techniques in their own way, but in the mid-twentieth century some composers took experimentation to extremes. Experimental and electronic music has changed the way audiences, performers and composers interact in a musical performance.

In the chapter on experimental and electronic music we shall look at the philosophies of several major experimental composers, exploring what they were trying to achieve in some of their experimental works. We shall also look at the rise of electronics in music and the work of one of electronic music's pioneers, Karlheinz Stockhausen (b.1928).

Expressionism and serialism

In this topic you will learn about:

- the difference between impressionism and expressionism
- the Second Viennese School
- how expressionism developed into serialism
- how to compose a piece of music using serial techniques.

Expressionist art

Look at the pictures below. One is by Claude Monet, an **impressionist** artist (*The Port at Argenteuil*) and the other by Ernst Ludwig Kirchner, an **expressionist** artist (*Self-portrait with a Model*).

Ernst Ludwig Kirchner, Self-portrait with a Model.

Claude Monet, The Port at Argenteuil.

What effect do the two pictures have on you? Does one make you feel more intense emotions than the other?

- Impressionist artists attempted to capture a moment or mood in their paintings, painting an *external* scene that moved them in some way.
- Expressionist artists attempted to express intense *internal* emotions, often with bold colours or distorted images.

Art and music have always been closely associated. The most important expressionist composer, Arnold Schoenberg (1874–1951), was also a painter and had close links with other artists and writers.

Glossary

expressionist term used to describe the highly emotional output of many artists, writers and composers at the start of the 20th century

impressionist term used to describe the paintings of Monet, Pissarro and others, which was later applied to the music of Debussy, Ravel and other composers who used musical colour in a way comparable to the painters

Social conditions of the early 1920s

The expressionist movement was strongest in Germany during the years immediately after the First World War. At this time, there was a strong feeling of disillusionment and discontent due to the after effects of the First World War, so the most intense emotions the artists, writers and composers wanted to express were generally related to these feelings. As such, works in the expressionist style tend to make us feel a little uncomfortable at times or, at the least, they are a little bit more difficult to digest than a typical impressionist work of the early 1900s.

1 Express yourself

a) Work in groups of three or four.

b) Take ten minutes to discuss the painting *Self-portrait with a Model*, listing any emotions it makes you feel (for example, fear, disgust, joy, longing and so on).

c) Experiment with ways to express these emotions using your instruments or voices. You *do not* need to worry about keys or even individual notes – if you can express the emotion best by randomly clicking flute keys or hitting the low notes of the piano very hard, then this is what you should use.

d) Experiment with combinations of sound instead of just playing one idea. For example, you may find that three people humming and gradually changing pitch is more effective than just one, or that the low clarinet notes combine particularly well with the muted bass guitar.

e) Structure your sounds into a piece lasting approximately one minute.

f) Perform and record your piece.

g) Listen back to the recording and list any ways you could change the piece to make it better reflect the painting.

h) Rehearse and re-record your piece with the changes you suggested.

Beyond tonality

Five Orchestral Pieces (1909) by Schoenberg is a set of pieces for full orchestra that do not use keys or relationships between keys in any way. They were some of the first completely **atonal** pieces ever written. In these works, Schoenberg used pitches and harmonies for effect rather than because of their relationship to each other. In most pieces written before this, composers normally employed a hierarchy of keys where one key, the **tonic**, would be the most important, followed by the dominant and relative major or minor and so on (see the 'Understanding music' chapter for more information on key relationships).

In *Five Orchestral Pieces*, Schoenberg is much more concerned with the combinations of **timbres** than with melody and harmony as we understand it. In a letter to a colleague he wrote, 'I have high expectations…particularly concerning sound and atmosphere. This is all that is important…a variegated, uninterrupted change of colours, rhythms and moods.'

Glossary

atonal music which is not in any key

timbre particular tone colour of an instrument or voice

tonic the first degree of a scale, the keynote

2 'Vorgefühle,' *Five Orchestral Pieces*, Schoenberg — CD1: 12

a) How does the piece reflect the title ('Vorgefühle' means 'Premonitions')? Think about:
- instrumental sounds in different combinations
- the pitch range of the instruments (**tessitura**)
- dynamic contrasts
- **textural** contrasts.

Glossary

tessitura the most commonly used part of the range of an instrument or voice

textural the number of parts in a piece of music and how they relate to one another

The Second Viennese School

Schoenberg began his composing career with several tonal pieces, continuing the traditions of Johannes Brahms (1833–97) and Richard Wagner (1813–83). Brahms was interested in writing music in strict forms (mostly borrowed from the Baroque and Classical eras) with Ludwig van Beethoven (1770–1827) as his role model, although his music was still very Romantic in scale. Wagner pushed tonality a long way from what audiences of the mid-1800s were used to through **chromaticism** and frequent key changes so that the key of a piece was often unclear. Wagner used perfect **cadences** in his

Glossary

cadence two chords at the end of a musical phrase. Four main types: perfect, imperfect, interrupted and plagal

chromaticism notes that are foreign to the key of the music. For example, sharps and flats in the key of C major would be chromatic notes

work much less than Classical composers such as Wolfgang Amadeus Mozart (1756–91) and Franz Joseph Haydn (1732–1809), preferring instead to keep the tension building.

Most composers of the early twentieth century had to react to what Brahms and Wagner had achieved, either by using Classical forms and key relationships in their own way or by abandoning them completely. Schoenberg came to the conclusion that music should be completely free from the restriction imposed by being in a key. He suggested that this was the way music must inevitably be written. 'Vorgefühle' from *Five Orchestral Pieces* is one of the examples of this approach – it is atonal. Schoenberg's move to atonal music coincided with a traumatic time in his life – his wife left him for one of his artist friends, who later committed suicide, and he was in severe financial difficulties, so he had a lot of intense emotions to express through his music!

Schoenberg's pupils, Anton Webern (1883–1945) and Alban Berg (1885–1935), took up the same style of composition as their teacher and together they came to be known as the 'Second Viennese School'.

Other composers also composed in an expressionist style for some of their careers, notably Paul Hindemith (1895–1963).

Serialism

It became clear to Schoenberg that it was very difficult to keep a piece going for any length of time if it did not contain the key relationships and cadences that contribute so much to the structure of music written up to this time. Since the central idea of Schoenberg's work was that there should not be a key (atonality), he had to find some other way to organize his ideas.

After some time experimenting, he arrived at his 'twelve tone technique' or, as he called it, 'method of composition with twelve notes which are related only with one another'. This involves taking the twelve available **semitones** in the octave and making a 'row' or 'series' by rearranging them in a particular order. Composers who adopted this technique were very careful about the exact nature of their basic series, concentrating on particular types of intervals (such as semitones or perfect fourths) so that these intervals occurred in their series more than any other. This technique is now called **serialism**.

Glossary

semitone half a note

serialism a compositional technique invented by Arnold Schoenberg and used by many composers of the 20th century

3 *String Quartet No. 4, 1st movement*, Schoenberg
CD1: 13

Listen to the first movement of Schoenberg's *String Quartet No. 4* (1936). Ask your teacher for a copy of the music score to accompany this task.

a) Describe the texture of the piece. Is it sparse or dense? Does it stay the same throughout?

b) Describe the pitch range of each instrument used in the piece (two violins, viola and cello). Is the range wide or does each instrument play in the middle of its register? Does the melody leap around a lot or does it mostly move by step?

c) Are the melodic lines easy to follow? Explain your answer.

d) To what extent are the harmonies dissonant or consonant?

e) Describe the dynamic range and how quickly the dynamics change.

f) Are there any rhythmic patterns that seem to be used more than any other? Describe the rhythms used in the piece using words such as broken/flowing, pulsing/gentle, quickly changing/similar throughout and so on.

Analysis of the prime row

The basic series used to compose Schoenberg's fourth string quartet is:

1	2	3	4	5	6	7	8	9	10	11	12
D	C#	A	B♭	F	E♭	E	C	A♭	G	F#	B

This is called the **prime row**, shortened to P_0.

Note how Schoenberg concentrated here on semitones and major thirds:

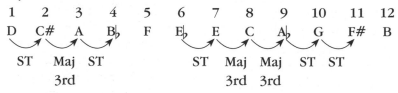

1	2	3	4	5	6	7	8	9	10	11	12
D	C#	A	B♭	F	E♭	E	C	A♭	G	F#	B

ST Maj ST   ST Maj Maj ST ST
    3rd   3rd 3rd

(ST = semitone, Maj 3rd = major third)

The prime row can be transformed in three ways:

- played backwards (**retrograde – R_0**)
- have all the intervals inverted (**inversion – I_0**)
- played backwards *and* have all the intervals inverted (**retrograde inversion – RI_0**).

	1	2	3	4	5	6	7	8	9	10	11	12
P_0	D	C#	A	B♭	F	E♭	E	C	A♭	G	F#	B
R_0	B	F#	G	A♭	C	E	E♭	F	B♭	A	C#	D
I_0	D	E♭	G	F#	B	C#	C	E	A♭	A	B♭	F
RI_0	F	B♭	A	A♭	E	C	C#	B	F#	G	E♭	D

Glossary

inversion (I_0) process of turning a part upside down, so that a mirror image is created to the original

prime row (P_0) the musical material on which a piece of serial music is based, normally consisting of the 12 notes of the chromatic scale in an order set by the composer (also known as the series, the note row or the tone row)

retrograde (R_0) a method of developing a series by reversing the order in which the pitches are heard

retrograde inversion (RI_0) a method of developing a series by reversing the order in which the pitches of the inverted series are heard

These four versions of the series can then each be transposed so that they start on any of the twelve available notes. For example, the prime row can be transposed up by two semitones – it would then be called P_2. If the starting note 'D' is transposed up two semitones, it would mean that P_2 begins on the note 'E'. The rest of the row is transposed in the same way:

	1	2	3	4	5	6	7	8	9	10	11	12
P_2	E	E♭	B	C	G	F	F#	D	B♭	A	A♭	C#

There can therefore be twelve versions of the prime row and each of its transformations: P_0–P_{11}. If the row were transposed up by twelve semitones, it would go back to the original (twelve semitones up from D is D again).

When serialism was applied strictly (notably by Schoenberg and Webern), all twelve notes of the row had to be used each time they appeared. Any note could be repeated and it was possible to use the pitches in any octave, but the entire row had to be used in order.

Chords could be formed by sounding several of the notes (in order) at the same time. This technique is known as **verticalisation**. In the example above (P_2), a three-note chord of E, E♭ and B could be formed (notes 1–3 of the row), or a four-note chord consisting of the pitches G, F, F# and D (notes 5–8 of the row). The pitches could be arranged in any order and in any octave within the chord itself. Obviously, most chords formed using this technique are very dissonant, but this is the idea. Some composers, such as Alban Berg, constructed rows that deliberately contained major and minor triads (for example, the notes G, B and D one after the other) so that there were some recognizable chords for audiences to grab hold of while listening.

When composers wrote out their pieces, they had to use a lot of accidentals. To avoid confusion they often used **enharmonic** versions of pitches (for example, A♭ is the same as G#).

Although the techniques described may seem quite mathematical, the composers were using them to come up with the basic themes for their pieces. They did not just put the twelve available semitones into a random order and then write them on the page along with a few transformations. Instead, they used the prime row like a classical composer would have used his main theme; the transformations are developments of the theme, but they have to be linked in a musical fashion, making use of dynamic contrast, the range of the available instruments and have some rhythmic motifs to go along with the pitches.

Glossary

enharmonic different ways of 'spelling' the same pitch, for example Bb and A#. One 'spelling' will make more harmonic sense than the other in tonal music, but the two are often interchangeable in atonal or highly chromatic music

verticalisation a method of producing chords in a serialist piece by playing adjacent notes of the series simultaneously

Serialism was a direct development from expressionism and the composers who used the technique were still trying to express intense inner emotions (this technique developed at the time of hyperinflation and famine in Germany in the early 1920s).

4 Composing a serial piece

a) Compose a row. Remember that this is not a random thing – the composers often gave more thought to this than to any other part of the composition.

    i) Decide on one or two intervals that you are going to concentrate on – for example, semitones, leaps of three semitones etc.

    ii) Decide what note you will start on.

    iii) Write out the twelve available semitones: A B♭ B C C# D E♭ E F F# G A♭.

    iv) Draw a grid with twelve columns and two rows like the one below:

1	2	3	4	5	6	7	8	9	10	11	12

    v) Fill each of the blank boxes with one note from the twelve available, crossing them out from your list as you put them in the boxes. Remember to try to use the intervals you have already decided on.

b) Draw a grid with thirteen columns and five rows and label it like the one below. Put your original row (P_0) into the first empty line as shown. The example row concentrates on semitones and leaps of five semitones (perfect fourths). Do not copy the example given – use your own row.

	1	2	3	4	5	6	7	8	9	10	11	12
P_0	F	B♭	A	D	E♭	A♭	G	F#	C#	C	B	E
R_0												
I_0												
RI_0|												

c) Reverse your original row by putting the note in box 12 into box 1, the note in box 11 into box 2, 10 into 3 and so on. In other words, write it backwards!

	1	2	3	4	5	6	7	8	9	10	11	12
P_0	F	B♭	A	D	E♭	A♭	G	F#	C#	C	B	E
R_0	E	B	C									

d) Transpose your original row. To do this you need to move *all* the notes up by the same amount of semitones. Follow the steps below.

  i) Write out the chromatic scale over two octaves as a guide.
  A B♭ B C C# D E♭ E F F# G A♭ A B♭ B C C# D E♭ E F F# G A♭

  ii) Decide on what interval you are going to transpose your row by (in the example, the row has been transposed up by five semitones).

  iii) In your 5 x 13 grid, label the fourth row 'P$_x$' (replace the 'x' with whatever your interval is).

  iv) Starting on the first note of your row, count up the number you have chosen. This is the first note of your transposed row.
  A B♭ B C C# D E (F) F# G A♭ A (B♭) B C C# D E♭ E F F# G A♭

  v) Repeat step (iv) for each note in your row, filling in your grid as you go along.

	1	2	3	4	5	6	7	8	9	10	11	12
P$_0$	F	B♭	A	D	E♭	A♭	G	F#	C#	C	B	E
R$_0$	E	B	C	C#	F#	G	A♭	E♭	D	A	B♭	F
P$_5$	B♭	E♭	D	G	A♭	C#	C	B	F#	F	E	A

e) Ask your teacher to check that your transposed row is accurate. You can also check it yourself; no notes should be used more than once in your transposed row – if any are, then you have made a mistake.

f) Reverse your transposed row the same way as you reversed the original row (the note in box 12 should move to box 1, 11 to 2 and so on).

	1	2	3	4	5	6	7	8	9	10	11	12
P$_0$	F	B♭	A	D	E♭	A♭	G	F#	C#	C	B	E
R$_0$	E	B	C	C#	F#	G	A♭	E♭	D	A	B♭	F
P$_5$	B♭	E♭	D	G	A♭	C#	C	B	F#	F	E	A
R$_5$	A	E	F	F#	B	C	C#	A♭	G	D	E♭	B♭

g) Now that all the 'themes' have been composed for your serial piece you need to compose some rhythmic motifs. You should make up three or four short rhythmic ideas like those below. Most of the ideas should use short durations, no longer than quavers, but one idea should have longer note values.

Motif 1	Motif 2	Motif 3	Motif 4

h) You need an overall structure for your piece. For this task we shall use binary form (AB). Choose two of the rows for section A and the other two for section B (for example, P$_0$ and R$_5$ for section A and P$_5$ and R$_0$ for section B).

i) You should write this piece for your own instrument so that you can make full use of your knowledge of the instrument's range and abilities. If you want to, you can write for two instruments so that you can move the rows from one part to the other.

j) Combine the pitches with the rhythms you have written, remembering all the points you made when you listened to the Schoenberg string quartet. You will need to count carefully to make sure you have given each bar its full value, and may need to use some odd rests depending on your rhythmic ideas. Your rhythms can cross the bar line if you wish.

k) Remember that you can repeat a note as many times as you want and you can use a note in any octave, but you should use all twelve notes of the row; do not use just notes 3–7, for example.

l) Try to think about the other aspects of your music as you write it out: dynamics, texture, instrumental range, tempo and so on. If you keep in mind an intense emotion that you are trying to express, just as you did with the earlier piece, you will be more successful.

m) Try inputting your piece into Sibelius, Cubase or whatever music software you have available. This will help if you need others to play it (you can print parts out) and will allow you to hear back your ideas. Serial music is often very difficult to perform; some pieces by the great serialist composers are so difficult to play that only the very best musicians even attempt them!

Further approaches to serialism

Many composers other than Schoenberg, Webern and Berg used serial techniques in their compositions, all in different ways to suit their own musical style. Composers made up rows using less than twelve notes or using odd combinations of tunings. Some composers used a serialist approach but applied it to tonal music – composing rows that belonged to a key.

Stravinsky used serialism in many of his pieces after the Second World War. Around this time, composers became interested in applying the technique to musical elements other than just pitches. Stockhausen (see pages 68–9) applied serial techniques to pitch, durations, dynamics and even timbre and **attack**. Composers who applied these techniques would make rhythmic rows, and rows controlling the dynamics from *pppp* (as soft as it is possible to play) to *ffff* (as loud as it is possible to play). After the initial rows had been composed, there remained little room for many more compositional decisions. Some criticized the approach as being much too restrictive. Webern said, however, that 'only on the basis of these [restrictions] has complete freedom become possible'. Whether you agree with him or not is a matter of personal opinion.

Glossary

attack the part of a sound that occurs immediately after it is sounded. The speed of the attack determines how quickly a note 'speaks': a sound which gradually fades in has a slow attack, but a sound which is very sudden has a fast attack

Minimalism

In this topic you will learn about:

- the origins of minimalism
- the major minimalist composers
- the elements that are commonly present in minimalist music
- how to compose a minimalist piece.

1 A little goes a long way

This is a task for the whole class. You are going to perform a piece that is different every time it is heard and changes according to what the performers decide to do. You might ask your teacher to record this unique event!

a) Split up into four groups (A, B, C and D) of equal size.

b) Your teacher will play the following four-note motif for you at a pitch suitable for the whole class.

c) Learn the motif and sing (or play) it over as a whole class.

d) The four groups should sing (or play) the motif in the following ways.

- Group A – sing or play only the first note of the motif (C), holding it for relatively long note values (at least four or five seconds). You may stop for a while at any point, but at least one member of the group should always be sounding the note while the piece continues.
- Group B – hum the second and third notes (E♭ and F), alternating between them as quickly or slowly as you wish.
- Group C – sing or play the motif, moving up or down at random, but by step only, for example C, E♭, F, E♭, C, E♭, F, G, F, G, F, E♭ and so on. Each note can be as long or short as you wish.
- Group D – sing or play the motif in ascending order only, but you may pause for as long as you like on each note.

e) Practise your part individually or as part of your small group.

f) The piece should be performed as follows.

i) Group A should walk around the classroom in a large circle.

ii) Groups B, C and D should walk within this large circle in a figure of eight shape.

iii) Group A should begin performing their drone and the other performers should enter when they decide it is time to do so.

iv) Any performer may stop singing/playing at any time (but keep moving!) and may rejoin the group at any time.

v) The piece ends with a gradual diminuendo, leaving only Group B humming their motif softly until they fade into silence. When the diminuendo starts, all performers should stop moving. When there is complete silence, try to hold the atmosphere for ten or twenty seconds by remaining completely still and silent.

g) It is important that you perform your own part without worrying about what anyone else does, but the idea is for everyone to experience the piece as a whole – to enjoy the overall sound – so listen carefully as you perform.

Origins of minimalism

Minimalism became popular in the United States of America in the 1960s after the experimental movement had made its mark on the world of music. It started out as part of the experimental genre itself, partly as a reaction to the rebirth of serialism in Western music.

After the death of Schoenberg in 1951, serialism again became very popular with composers. Many minimalist composers began their composing careers by writing serial music. However, they found that this method of composing music did not allow them to express themselves in the way they wanted.

Task 1 contains elements of the main principles of minimalism (**drone**, **repetition** and **phasing**) and elements of experimental music (elements in the composition that are decided by the performers, adjusting their sound production to suit what they hear around them). Early minimalist pieces and many by composers who were later acknowledged as 'minimalists' were experimental in nature. For example, Steve Reich's *Pendulum Music* (1968) involves four microphones swinging back and forth in front of some amplifiers, creating intentional feedback.

La Monte Young and Terry Riley

La Monte Young is thought to be the first composer to write in the style that was later called 'minimalism'. He was completely fascinated with drones and repetition. He studied Indian and Japanese music (he was also intrigued by the sound of the wind and electrical hum!), and started to use drones as the basis of his music.

Glossary

drone a sustained sound

phasing when two or more versions of a sound or musical motif are played simultaneously but slightly out of synchronisation.
Often this is used as a development technique in minimalism where the start points of the motifs will gradually converge after a period of time

repetition the restatement of a section of music – maybe just a few notes or even a whole section of music

Not many of Young's pieces have been recorded because he feels they are never really complete. He has been developing his most famous work, *The Tortoise: His Dreams and Journeys,* since 1964, constantly changing and adding to it. The basic idea is that players and singers add harmonics to a note produced on a synthesizer, dropping in and out, much like you did in your performance in Task 1, but in a very closely controlled fashion.

Terry Riley (b.1935) was a friend and colleague of Young's. He studied with Young and his career as a composer shadowed Young's for a while. In the early 1960s, Riley experimented with tape loops of various sounds, combining these with delay and occasional instrumental sounds. He would run the loops through the reel-to-reel tape recorders, out of the open window, around some wine bottles and back in to the tape recorder again. Steve Reich took these experiments with tape loops slightly further.

Riley was a solo performer, playing many concerts using an electronic organ, a soprano saxophone and some echo devices. He would set up a drone with the electronic organ and improvise on the saxophone, exploring motifs he had written down in shorthand. The echo devices would help him to build up textures that would give the sound of more than one performer and involved much repetition of musical material.

Riley's most important work, which brought minimalism to the notice of the musical mainstream, was *In C*, written in 1965. This piece focuses on the repetition of short musical fragments along with a constantly repeating quaver C keeping the pulse.

Steve Reich

While Young is considered to be the founder of minimalism, Steve Reich and Philip Glass are probably the most important minimalist composers. They studied together and started composing in a minimalist style around the same time, but they have always been more rivals than friends.

'The process of change' was Reich's main concern. He wanted the listener to be aware of the gradual changes occurring in the music. His pieces tend to be long and, to appreciate his musical philosophy, you need to listen to the whole piece.

In 1966, Reich stumbled across a phenomenon called phasing. He had recorded a black preacher on a street corner and selected a phrase he found musically interesting.

He made two identical tape loops of the phrase 'It's gonna rain' and ran them simultaneously on identical tape recorders. Due to tiny differences in the motor speeds of the two machines, one loop gradually went out of sync with the other. Over the space of about seven minutes, the two loops eventually came back into sync (or 'in phase'). At the start of the piece, Reich manipulates the loops by cutting them into smaller lengths and splicing them together, creating an effect similar to that achieved by DJs when they **scratch** records.

Glossary

scratch a sound produced by manually spinning a vinyl disk at a different speed than originally intended (backwards or forwards) while the needle is in contact with the disk

2 *Time Becomes*, Orbital

CD1: 14

Time Becomes by Orbital (1993) demonstrates the principles of Reich's tape loop pieces. After the brief introduction (Spock instructing members of the Starship *Enterprise* about a theory concerning the Moebius in the series *Star Trek*), the piece consists only of two loops of the same phrase 'where time becomes a loop'. One loop is very slightly longer than the other, so each time it repeats, it sounds a little later than before. The result is a phasing effect where the loops gradually move out of sync with each other and then, as the piece progresses, come back into sync again.

a)   Describe the phasing phenomenon with reference to the rhythm of the speech.

Minimalism in art

The phenomenon of hearing something not originally intended by the composer as a result of shifting musical textures has a direct equivalent in the visual arts. In the etching opposite, the artist, Kate Whiteford, has combined a series of broken vertical lines to produce an effect that goes beyond the simple original idea. The longer you look at the works, the more you can see. Minimalist and conceptual works of art are intended to be looked at over a long period of time so the viewer makes their own interpretation of the work.

Kate Whiteford, Crossing the Line.

Instrumental minimalism

Reich did not just use mechanical means to perform his phasing concept. The piece *Piano Phase* (1967) involves two performers playing a short phrase and gradually going out of sync with each other. He later developed the concept for larger ensembles and other groups of instruments.

Many twentieth-century composers, including minimalists, have been influenced by music from around the world. In the early 1970s, Reich travelled to Africa and Indonesia to study with some of the great musicians of these cultures. His interest in **polyrhythms** and tuned percussion was reinforced by these trips, resulting in pieces such as *Drumming* (1971) and *Music for Eighteen Musicians* (1975–6).

Philip Glass was heavily influenced by the rhythmic cycles, **ragas** and drones of Indian music after he spent some time in the mid-60s travelling in India and the Middle East. Neither Reich nor Glass tried to recreate the sounds of these cultures using Western instruments; they just absorbed some of the principles of the music into their own styles.

When Reich composed pieces using polyrhythms, he often used very short rhythmic ideas that he could later expand on by gradually adding notes. He would combine several of these ideas to make a piece sound rhythmically complicated, even though the individual rhythms were very simple.

The harmonies in his pieces tended to be **diatonic**. He did use some dissonances, but these were either repeated a great deal so that the ear became accustomed to them, or they formed part of a lush chord so they did not sound too harsh. **Modes** and **major** scales were commonly used by Reich as a basis for his harmonies.

Glossary

diatonic notes belonging to or literally 'of the key'

major western tonal music in bright sounding keys. A major key has four semitones between the first and third notes (C-E)

modes precursors of modern scales. There are seven different modes

motifs short melodic or rhythmic ideas used as a basis for manipulation and development in a musical composition

polyrhythms two or more different rhythms played together

raga improvised music in several contrasting sections, based on a series of notes from a particular rag

3 Many rhythms make light work

In this task you will compose several rhythmic **motifs** that you can use later in the chapter for the main composition task.

a) Play through the following four scales and decide which you want to use in your piece. You can transpose it up or down later if you wish, but for now they all start on 'C' for simplicity.

Major scale	C	D	E	F	G	A	B
Mixolydian mode	C	D	E	F	G	A	B♭
Lydian mode	C	D	E	F#	G	A	B
Major pentatonic scale	C	D	E		G	A	

b) Draw a grid with nine columns and five rows like the one below. Label the rows 1–5.

c) In the fifth row, fill in six of the boxes using notes from your chosen scale. You do not have to use all of the notes and you can repeat notes if you wish. In the example, the mixolydian mode has been used.

1								
2								
3								
4								
5	C			G	A	B♭	G	G	

d) Copy row 5 into row 4, but leave out one of the notes so that there are only five boxes filled in instead of six. In the example below, the third note, G, has been left out.

1								
2								
3								
4	C			A	B♭	G	G		
5	C		G	A	B♭	G	G		

e) Copy row 4 into row 3, leaving out one of the notes so that there are only four boxes filled in. In the example below, the final G has been left out.

1								
2								
3	C			A	B♭	G			
4	C			A	B♭	G	G		
5	C		G	A	B♭	G	G		

f) Continue with the same procedure until all the rows have been completed, with only two boxes of the top row filled in.

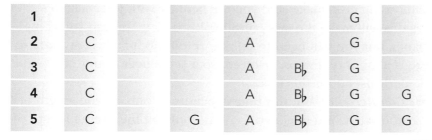

1			A		G	
2	C		A		G	
3	C		A	B♭	G	
4	C		A	B♭	G	G
5	C	G	A	B♭	G	G

g) Repeat stages b–f so that you have a second grid. You should use the same scale as you did for the first grid, but your choice of notes should be different, as should be the boxes where you place them.

h) Repeat stages b–f one more time so that you end up with three contrasting grids.

In your grid, each box represents a quaver duration. Each empty box represents a quaver rest, so there are a lot of rests in the first few rows. The process of starting with a short motif (as in row 1) and gradually adding to it is called **note addition**. The same thing can be done in reverse – you can start out by playing a motif with few rests in it and gradually subtract notes. This process, called **note subtraction**, would normally be used towards the end of a piece.

Glossary

note addition a method of developing cells in minimalist music by gradually adding notes to the original cell

note subtraction a method of developing cells in minimalist music by gradually taking notes away from the original cell

4 *Electric Counterpoint, 1st movement*, Steve Reich CD1: 15

The central section of the first movement of *Electric Counterpoint* (1988) is derived from a Central African horn music motif Reich learned on his travels. The outside sections contain a pulsing idea. He uses the pulses to make the slow moving chords much more interesting. Each one lasts approximately the same length as a long breath.

Listen to the piece twice.
a) On the first hearing, just listen to how the gradual changes are introduced.
b) On the second hearing, see if you can spot the following:
- pulsing chords (giving a hypnotic effect)
- gradual addition/subtraction of instruments
- fading in and out (dynamic contrast, but gradual and controlled)
- layering of melodic fragments (motifs)
- addition of notes to melodic motifs
- complex rhythms built up by layering several different, simple, rhythmic motifs
- fading one idea out while fading another in
- importance of accents in the rhythmic motifs.

5 Minimum material, maximum impact

Before attempting this composing task, make sure you are familiar with your school's sequencing equipment, as this will make the task considerably easier. You can still complete the task using pen and paper, but you will need to think carefully about who you want to perform your piece. There is a lot of repetition involved, so a sequencer's copy and paste functions would be particularly useful for this task.

a) Listen again to *Electric Counterpoint*, but this time concentrate only on the length of each section. Time it with a stopwatch. You might concentrate only on the overall length of the major sections (the two outside pulsing sections and the middle African motif section), or you might go even further and time how long the composer lets one chord or one motif last before changing it. Use these timings as a guideline for your own piece (you can divide the lengths in half if you wish).

b) Draw a timeline along the edge of an A4 piece of paper. It should last three to six minutes. Make a mark to represent every ten seconds.

c) Along the short edge of the paper, write the numbers 1–5 to represent the individual instruments that will be playing the piece.

d) Now think of the sounds you are going to use. Most of them should be percussive in nature. One should be capable of sustaining notes and another capable of playing more than one note at a time. Instruments 1–3 will use the grids you composed in Task 3 on page 52–3.

e) Divide your timeline into three sections. Each section will concentrate on a different way to combine your chosen instruments.

f) Decide on when each of your five instruments will be playing, shading in alongside the instrument number when it will be playing on the timeline. You are deciding on the texture of the piece here by altering the number of instruments playing at any given time. Remember that you should try to make the changes in texture gradual, and you should include a build and fall in texture somewhere in your piece (at least once each). Minimalist pieces often (but not always) start a section with a thin texture, build up towards the centre and thin out towards the end. Instrument 5 should play most of the way through this piece.

g) Using only notes from the scale you chose in Task 3, create a three- or four-note chord that you like the sound of. This will be used for 'pulsing' effects. This can be played by a combination of instruments or by the instrument capable of playing more than one note.

h) Create a second chord in the same way, which complements the one you created in stage g.

i) Now that you have your structure and the majority of your musical ideas, you need to combine the two.

    i) Using the grids from Task 3, grid 1 will be the musical material for instrument 1, grid 2 for instrument 2 and grid 3 for instrument 3. Start by arranging these ideas according to your structure 'map'. You may have to alter either your structure map or your grids while trying to make this fit, but that is part of the composing process.

    ii) The instruments play the grids by starting on line 1, repeating this line a number of times, then moving on to line 2, repeating this a number of times, moving on to line 3 and so on.

iii) Instrument 5 will be the instrument (or combination of instruments) playing the chords. There are several suggestions for arranging your chords below.

- One chord 'pulses' by being repeated every quaver or semiquaver.
- One chord 'pulses' by playing two notes on one quaver and the other note(s) on the next quaver.
- You alternate between one chord and the other every bar or every quaver.
- You use the first chord for sections 1 and 3 and the second chord for section 2.
- You play the chord over a long note, swelling in from *pianissimo* to *mezzo forte* to *pianissimo* again.
- Combine any of the above or use your own ideas based on minimalist music you have listened to.

j) Use instrument 4 to phase with the grid most prominent at the time; it should play the same motif, but either add or drop a quaver (so that it is nine or seven quavers long). This way it will take either seven or nine repetitions to come back into phase again.

C		G	A		B♭	G	G	C		G	A		B♭	G	G	C		G	A		B♭	G	G
C		G	A		B♭	G	C		G	A		B♭	G	C		G	A		B♭	G	C		G

An example of phasing – the top row is the eight-quaver motif repeated and the bottom row is the same motif but with the last quaver taken out, making it a seven-quaver motif.

k) Repetition is vital to minimalist music. Your motifs become **ostinati** when they are continuously repeated. Do not be afraid to repeat each line of the grids up to ten or twelve times if it seems appropriate. Also, if the resulting sound is more pleasing, you might want to play a grid in reverse order, starting at line 5 and working back to line 1.

Glossary

ostinato a repeated rhythm, melody or chord pattern

l) Gradual changes in dynamics are vital to keep interest in your piece. Apply these as seems appropriate. Listen again to *Electric Counterpoint* to hear how Reich uses dynamic contrast.

m) Remember that this is *your* composition. You can change any of the ideas to suit your own tastes – they are not rules.

- If, in performance of your music, you feel that something should be lengthened or shortened, do so.
- If you feel a part does not fit where you originally put it, move it.
- If you think a note should be changed in your grid, do so.
- Would a different instrument sound better than the one you chose originally? If so, change it.
- Would it be better if you had another instrument playing something else? Add the extra instrument.
- Is it too messy because of too many parts? Take one out.

You have the freedom to do anything you think will improve your piece.

Philip Glass

Glossary

arpeggio the sounding of the tones of a chord in rapid succession rather than simultaneously

triad a three note chord ('tri' means three)

Philip Glass has a very lyrical, accessible style, but his music still belongs to the minimalist genre. It is deceptively simple, often including long passages of alternating notes and repeated broken chords (often as basic as major or minor **arpeggios**), but the genius of his music is in knowing just how long is long enough. He precisely notates his music, in keeping with traditional composers, so there is never any doubt about the number of repetitions in a section.

Glass is well known as the only minimalist composer to be seriously involved in theatre and opera. He has written many operas, the most famous being *Einstein on the Beach* (1975–6). His operas have been criticized because they rarely follow a plot. He signed a deal with the major record label CBS (later to become Sony Classical), which distributed his music to a wide audience. As a result he has become one of the most famous living composers.

Until the time of serialism in the early twentieth century, composers were very concerned about relationships between chords and keys. Glass has a highly individual approach to harmony – he uses the straightforward **triads**, but they often have little relationship to one another except that the notes are close together on the keyboard. Look at the opening chord sequence from his 1981 piece *Facades*, shown below:

	A min	A♭ maj	A♭ (#4)	A min	B♭ maj	B♭ min	A min
Part 1	C	C	D	C	D	D	C
Part 1	A	A♭	A♭	A	B♭	B♭	A
Part 2	E	E♭	E♭	E	F	F	E
Part 2	A	A♭	A♭	A	B♭	B♭	A

Part 1 alternates between the top two notes and part 2 alternates between the bottom two notes. The individual parts change very little and, when they do, the notes they change to are very close in terms of their position on the keyboard.

6 *Violin Concerto, 1st movement*, Philip Glass

Listen to the first movement of the *Violin Concerto* (1987) by Philip Glass.

a) List the minimalist techniques you can hear being used in this piece.

b) Has Glass used the alternating note idea or the triad arpeggio idea in the solo violin when it first enters?

c) What percussion instruments can you hear?

d) List three words that best describe the use of the brass instruments in this piece.

e) Compare this piece to *Electric Counterpoint*. What similarities can you hear?

Beyond minimalism

Although John Adams (b.1947) has declared himself a 'post-minimalist' composer, he is considered to be one of the major composers of the minimalist style. His approach combines some of the rhythmic complexity of Steve Reich with the small-scale repetition of Philip Glass. His music is generally for traditional ensembles, often quite large orchestras. It is felt to be minimalist because of the use of repetition and the often quite static harmony. One of his most famous works, *Tromba Lontana* (1986), displays both of these qualities.

Like Glass, Adams also composed some opera and is concerned with the commercial success of his work. His music is often more accessible than that of Young, Riley or Reich, but can be much more dissonant than Glass's work.

Minimalism has inspired many composers and musicians outside of Western Classical music. For example, when Steve Reich moved on from his extreme use of repetition and the very gradual process of change in the late 1970s, Brian Eno commented that this was 'rather fortunate because that meant I could carry on with it'. Eno later developed the style into ambient music (*Music for Airports*, written in 1978, is one of the most important ambient works), which in turn influenced bands like The Orb and Orbital to develop their loop-based dance music styles.

Experimental and electronic music

In this topic you will learn about how:

- experimental composers approached composition
- to go about composing a piece of experimental music
- to create a graphic score
- the roles of performer and composer became less defined.

1 *4'33"*, John Cage

This piece can be performed by any number of musicians. It is an experimental piece in which the emphasis is on background noise. The idea is to have a live performance where the audience listens to all the shuffling, coughing, lights, traffic noise and so on. It can be of any length, although the most famous performance lasted a total of 4 minutes and 33 seconds (David Tudor – piano, 1952), hence the title. In that performance, Tudor marked the different movements by opening the piano lid at the start and closing it at the end of a movement.

a) Prepare yourself with your instrument as you would normally, sitting or standing ready for a performance.

b) Perform and listen to the following score and make a recording:

Movement I – Tacet (silent)

Movement II – Tacet

Movment III – Tacet

c) Now, listen to the recording you made.
   i)   What did you hear?
   ii) Did you realize all those sounds were present as you entered the room?
   iii) What did you feel during the performance?

Aleatoric music

Any given performance of *4'33"* is unique, depending on the environment in which it is performed. If it is performed in the dead of winter in a large concert hall, there might be a few sniffles and muted coughs, the sound of the heating system starting up, rain on the auditorium roof and so on. Of course, these sounds would be present in a performance of any piece of music in the form of background noise; it is just that Cage made the **environmental noise** the music.

4'33" is one of the most famous examples of **aleatoric** music (chance music) or, to use the label Cage himself gave it, **indeterminacy**.

In the case of aleatoric music, we are not concerned about the melody, harmony or rhythm of the piece, or even if it has any beauty or emotional content that might make it worthwhile. The piece will be considered successful if it makes the audience experience something within them, which is brought about by the performance.

Did you experience anything while listening to *4'33"*? Perhaps a sense of unease, anticipation or heightened awareness of things going on around you. If so, then the piece was successful because you had nothing to respond to except your own expectation of what was about to be performed.

Glossary

aleatoric music in which some aspects of composition or realisation are left to chance

environmental noise background noise, such as that made by traffic outside an auditorium or the humming of electrical equipment

indeterminacy music in which some or all aspects of composition and realisation are left to chance

2 *4'33"*, John Cage

a) Now you understand a little about Cage's philosophy, try performing *4'33"* again.

b) Use a different combination of instruments – does this make a difference to your perceptions of the piece?

John Cage

John Cage (1912–1992) did not begin his composing career with aleatoric music – it was a philosophy he adopted after much experimentation. Originally he was taught by Schoenberg, the inventor of **serialism**, and he wrote several pieces using serial techniques. He found that he preferred to use noise in a musical context, so he started experimenting a great deal with percussion ensembles. Once, when asked to write a piece for a dance performance, he decided to write a piece for percussion ensemble. Unfortunately the theatre was equipped with a piano and had room for little else, certainly not a percussion ensemble. To get around the problem, Cage inserted various objects (such as pieces of rubber, screws, and nuts and bolts) into the strings of the piano at specific points. The effect was to turn the piano into a percussion ensemble!

Cage was very pleased with the concept of his 'prepared piano' and used it for many works in the 1940s. His interest in Eastern philosophy (particularly Zen Buddhism) and Indonesian gamelan music could be expressed much more easily with the prepared piano than with any other Western instrument.

Cage did not care much about pitch or harmony in his prepared piano works – he was much more interested in timbre. Therefore he could not use key relationships as a way to structure his pieces, as was the case with composers until the end of the nineteenth century. In his major work for prepared piano, *Sonatas and Interludes for Prepared Piano* (1946–8), each piece is in binary form. Within this, the sections (divided by double bar lines) are all in some numerical ratio to each other. The numerical relationship is obvious and is central to the piece. Cage treated this play on numbers as his main structural device.

Within the individual phrases, the music is quite free flowing, but it is very hard to relate the music to the score because of the preparations.

The music is notated quite precisely. This is not an example of aleatoric music because there is no element of chance involved beyond the possibility of slightly different sounds from minor differences between instruments. The performer interprets the piece much as they would any traditional piece of piano music with the added complication of the preparation. Cage wrote the piece you will listen to in Task 3 before he started moving towards his philosophy of indeterminacy.

Glossary

serialism a compositional technique invented by Arnold Schoenberg and used by many composers of the 20th century

3 'Sonata for prepared piano, No. 5', *Sonatas and Interludes for Prepared Piano*, John Cage

CD1: 17

This piece is represented by standard musical notation with an additional sheet for instructions on how to 'prepare' the piano.

Tone	Material	Strings left to right	Distance from damper (inches)	Material	Strings left to right	Distance from damper (inches)	Material	Strings left to right	Distance from damper (inches)	Tone
				Screw	2–3	$1\frac{1}{4}$ *				A
				Med. Bolt	2–3	$1\frac{3}{8}$ *				G
				Screw	2–3	$1\frac{5}{8}$ *				F
				Screw	2–3	$1\frac{13}{16}$ *				E
				Screw	2–3	$1\frac{3}{4}$ *				E♭
				Sm. Bolt	2–3	2 *				D
				Screw	2–3	$1\frac{11}{16}$ *				C♯
				Furniture Bolt	2–3	$2\frac{3}{16}$ *				C
16va				Screw	2–3	$2\frac{1}{2}$ *				B
				Screw	2–3	$1\frac{7}{8}$ *				B♭
				Med. Bolt	2–3	$2\frac{3}{8}$ *				A
				Screw	2–3	$2\frac{1}{4}$				A♭
				Screw	2–3	$3\frac{1}{4}$ *				G
				Screw	2–3	$2\frac{15}{16}$ *				F♯
	Screw	1–2	$3\frac{3}{4}$ *	Furn. Bolt + 2 Nuts	2–3	$2\frac{1}{4}$ *	Screw + 2 Nuts	2–3	$3\frac{3}{4}$ *	F
				Screw	2–3	$1\frac{13}{16}$ *				E
				Furniture Bolt	2–3	$1\frac{7}{8}$				E♭
				Screw	2–3	$1\frac{15}{16}$				C♯
				Screw	2–3	$1\frac{7}{16}$				C
8va	(Damper to bridge = $4\frac{7}{16}$; adjust accordingly)			Med. Bolt	2–3	$3\frac{3}{4}$				B
				Screw	2–3	$4\frac{7}{16}$				A
	Rubber	1–2–3	$4\frac{1}{2}$	Furniture Bolt	2–3	$1\frac{1}{4}$				G♯
				Screw	2–3	$1\frac{3}{4}$				F♯
				Screw	2–3	$2\frac{5}{16}$				F
	Rubber	1–2–3	$5\frac{3}{4}$							E
	Rubber	1–2–3	$6\frac{1}{2}$	Furn. Bolt + Nut	2–3	$6\frac{7}{8}$				E♭
				Furniture Bolt	2–3	$2\frac{9}{16}$				D
	Rubber	1–2–3	$5\frac{5}{8}$							D♭
				Bolt	2–3	$7\frac{1}{8}$				C
				Bolt	2–3	2				B
	Screw	1–2	10	Screw	2–3	1	Rubber	1–2–3	$8\frac{1}{4}$	B♭
	(Plastic (see G))	1–2–3	$2\frac{15}{16}$				Rubber	1–2–3	$4\frac{1}{2}$	G♯
	Plastic (over 1 under 2–3)	1–2–3	$2\frac{7}{8}$				Rubber	1–2–3	$10\frac{1}{8}$	G
	(Plastic (see D))	1–2–3	$4\frac{1}{4}$				Rubber	1–2–3	$5\frac{7}{16}$	D♯
	Plastic (over 1 under 2–3)	1–2–3	$4\frac{1}{8}$				Rubber	1–2–3	$9\frac{3}{4}$	D
	Bolt	1–2	$15\frac{1}{2}$	Bolt	2–3	$\frac{11}{16}$	Rubber	1–2–3	$14\frac{1}{8}$	D♭
	Bolt	1–2	$14\frac{1}{2}$	Bolt	2–3	$\frac{7}{8}$	Rubber	1–2–3	$6\frac{1}{2}$	C
	Bolt	1–2	$14\frac{3}{4}$	Bolt	2–3	$\frac{9}{16}$	Rubber	1–2–3	14	B
	Rubber	1–2–3	$9\frac{1}{2}$	Med. Bolt	2–3	$10\frac{1}{8}$				B♭
	Screw	1–2	$5\frac{7}{8}$	Lg. Bolt	2–3	$5\frac{7}{8}$	Screw + Nuts	1–2	1	A
	Bolt	1–2	$7\frac{1}{8}$	Med. Bolt	2–3	$2\frac{1}{4}$	Rubber	1–2–3	$4\frac{1}{8}$	A♭
	Long Bolt	1–2	$8\frac{3}{4}$	Lg. Bolt	2–3	$3\frac{3}{4}$				G
				Bolt	2–3	$\frac{11}{16}$				D
8va bass	Screw + Rubber	1 2	$4\frac{7}{16}$							D
16va bass	Eraser (over D under C + E♭)	1	$6\frac{3}{4}$							D

* Measure from bridge.

John Cage: *Sonatas and Interludes*. Edition Peters No. 6755 © 1960 by Henmar Press Inc., New York
Reproduced by permission of Peters Edition Limited, London.

a) Which instruments do you think Cage has tried to recreate using his prepared piano? List the 'instruments' you think you can hear.

b) Has Cage grouped the 'instruments' in different ways? For example, does one type of sound use faster notes than another?

Use of new or unconventional sounds

Experimental composers were not the first to experiment with different ways of producing sound from conventional instruments. Gustav Holst (1874–1934) used the **col legno** bowing technique in 'Mars' from *The Planets* suite, and flamenco guitarists have always used the body of the guitar as a percussion device to accompany their music.

In fact, most of the great composers embraced any progress in instrument manufacture and sometimes they invented new instruments themselves to produce the sound they needed for a particular composition (for example, in the mid-1800s, Richard Wagner invented an instrument that is a cross between a tuba and a French horn called the 'Wagner tuba'). When the celeste was invented, Peter Tchaikovsky (1840–93) did his very best to hide it from his rival, Nicholas Rimsky-Korsakov (1844–1908), so that he could be the first to use its delicate sound (it was used in 'Dance of the Sugar-Plum Fairy' from the ballet *The Nutcracker*).

Glossary

col legno in string music, this means to be played with the wood of the bow

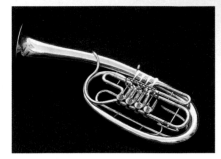

The Wagner tuba is just one example of experimentation with musical instruments.

Noise as music

The genre 'experimental music' takes in elements of indeterminacy, avant-garde music, pre-twentieth-century music and electronic music, but the focus is always on finding a new way to compose or express a musical idea. It does not normally hide the experimental element beneath traditional harmonies and structures, but glories in the newness and alien nature of the experimentation.

An example of this is *Memories of You* (1964) by Cornelius Cardew (1936–81). This piece is written for grand piano and three objects of the performer's choice with which to make noise. In the recording you will hear in Task 4, the performer chose a paperback copy of some music, a pencil and his hand as the three objects.

The score consists of a 'map' that directs the performer to make various noises on, in or around the piano. The exact nature of the noises is left to the performer to decide. In this recording, the paper rustling and playing of the inside of the piano can be heard quite clearly – not activities normally associated with a traditional piano piece! This piece would sound different every time it is performed or recorded – the directions on the score are not exact, being left open to the performer's interpretation. This element of the performer taking some of the responsibility for the completion of the composition is very important in some experimental music.

4 *Memories of You*, Cornelius Cardew

CD1: 18

Listen to *Memories of You* by Cornelius Cardew.

a) Do you think it is effective as a piece of music? Give reasons for your answer.

b) Compare Cage's *4'33"* with *Memories of You*. Which uses noise most effectively? Why?

Graphic notation

Traditional staff notation failed to meet the extreme demands that experimental composers made of it, so composers had to find another way to represent their music so that others could perform it. They found that the most suitable format involved some sort of graphic representation of the sound, resulting in a **graphic score**.

Cardew and other experimental composers adopted graphic scores for several reasons.

- They gave the performer more freedom when interpreting the symbols than would be true of staff (traditional) notation.
- Many of the sounds in the compositions could not be notated using only staff notation.
- They wanted to enable *anyone* to perform their pieces, especially those with no musical training and therefore unlikely to be able to read music.

However, it turned out that many performers struggled to make any sort of sense out of some of the scores Cardew produced. He spent several years preparing his masterpiece *Treatise* (1963–7). This work consisted of 193 pages of graphic score with no explanation of how to interpret the various symbols. After several performances of this work, Cardew decided that most musicians were 'visual innocents and ignoramuses' (he felt they struggled to interpret graphic symbols), so he had to look for another way of notating his works. The result was a text-based approach, developed on the assumption that most people can read, therefore they can perform the music whether they are musically trained or not. In fact, Cardew considered a musical training to be an obstacle to interpreting his pieces rather than a help.

Glossary

graphic score a visual representation of a piece of music which does not need to include any traditional form of musical notation. Often a significant amount of interpretation is required by the performer in order to realise the score

Some have said that Cardew was 'gleefully experimental' when he was writing *Memories of You*. Adopt the same attitude when you attempt the next task. Have fun writing it and abandon any thoughts of making it sound like a traditional piece of music!

5 What can you get out of your instrument?

How can you produce sound from your instrument other than the conventional ways that you have been taught?

a) Experiment and make a list of your five favourite sounds. Include on your list instructions for how to produce these sounds so that another performer could do so without having to ask you. Remember that you are not concerned here with pitch, or even with making 'nice' sounds – you are experimenting to see what is possible with your instrument. If your instrument is your voice, follow the instructions in exactly the same way that an instrumentalist would – consider your mouth, nose, chest and throat to be the physical instrument.

b) Find some ways to develop your five sounds. For example, if scraping the plectrum up and down the guitar strings created one sound, you could alter it by scraping different strings, changing the length and speed of the scrape, using different materials to scrape the strings with and so on.

c) Create some symbols, icons or words to represent the individual sounds. Symbols that represent developments of each sound should obviously relate to the symbol for the original sound.

d) List your sounds on separate pieces of paper. Underneath the sound, list all the developments of the sounds that you can think of.

Structuring experimental music

How can you combine the sounds of experimental music to make a unified piece of music? Obviously the normal rules of harmony and structure do not apply here, so you need to use some new ways of thinking.

Experimental composers often used paintings, architecture, poetry and other non-musical stimuli to help them structure their music. Cage used mathematical formulae to structure his prepared piano pieces.

The activity on page 66 aims to demonstrate how a non-musical score can be used to give structure to a composition.

6 Organizing sound

a) Choose some form of non-musical source as the stimulus for the structure of your piece (for example, a painting).

b) Organize the sounds to best represent this structure (for example, if the painting is sparse but brightly coloured, the sounds should be sparse, but intense). Remember to keep the piece playable. If you want to do two things at once, each of which requires both hands, you will need to write the piece as a duet or else re-think the sound combinations.

c) Carefully construct a graphic score for your piece. This should contain your symbols/icons/words, but does not have to be in a traditional read-from-left-to-right order.

d) Consider the following points when constructing your graphic score.
   - Would it be better arranged in a circle or spiral?
   - Are you going to give the performer(s) the choice of where to begin?
   - What would happen if a performer on a different instrument (especially one from a different instrumental family) were to try interpreting your symbols?
   - Could you have two or three performers on different (or the same) instruments starting from different points in the score?

Note that if you are to submit this piece as a GCSE composition, you will need to accompany it with detailed notes on what your intentions were and how you developed your initial ideas.

7 'Paragraph 7', *The Great Learning*, Cornelius Cardew

→ sing 8   IF
sing 5   THE ROOT
sing 13 (f 3)   BE IN CONFUSION
sing 6   NOTHING
sing 5 (f 1)   WILL
sing 8   BE
sing 8   WELL
sing 7   GOVERNED
hum 7
→ sing 8   THE SOLID
sing 8   CANNOT BE
sing 9 (f 2)   SWEPT AWAY
sing 8   AS
sing 17 (f 1)   TRIVIAL
sing 6   AND
sing 8   NOR
sing 8   CAN
sing 17 (f 1)   TRASH
sing 8   BE ESTABLISHED AS
sing 9 (f 2)   SOLID
sing 5 (f 1)   IT JUST
sing 4   DOES NOT
sing 6 (f 1)   HAPPEN
hum 3 (f 2)
→ speak 1   MISTAKE NOT CLIFF FOR
MORASS AND TREACHEROUS BRAMBLE

NOTATION
→ The leader gives a signal and all enter concertedly at the same moment. The second of these signals is optional; those wishing to observe it should gather to the leader and choose a new note and enter just as at the beginning (see below).
"sing 9 (f 2) SWEPT AWAY" means: sing the words "SWEPT AWAY" on a length-of-a-breath note (syllables freely disposed) nine times; the same note each time; of the nine notes two (any two) should be loud, the rest soft. After each note take in breath and sing again.
"hum 7" means: hum a length-of-a-breath note seven times; the same note each time; all soft.
"speak 1" means: speak the given words in steady tempo all together, in a low voice, once (follow the leader).

PROCEDURE
Each chorus member chooses his own note (silently) for the first line (if eight times). All enter together on the leader's signal. For each subsequent line choose a note that you can hear being sung by a colleague. It may be necessary to move to within earshot of certain notes. The note, once chosen, must be carefully retained. Time may be taken over the choice. If there is no note, or only the note you have just been singing, or only a note or notes that you are unable to sing, choose your note for the next line freely. Do not sing the same note on two consecutive lines.
Each singer progresses through the text at his own speed. Remain stationary for the duration of a line; move around only between lines.
All must have completed "hum 3 (f 2)" before the signal for the last line is given. At the leader's discretion this last line may be omitted.

'Paragraph 7' from *The Great Learning* by Cornelius Cardew. Copyright: Horace Cardew

Each performance of *The Great Learning* (1968–70) will be completely unique, but that is part of the philosophy behind the piece. The text-based score allows anyone who can sing to attempt a performance. The instructions leave a lot of space for interpretation and chance, but it is much easier to follow than a graphic score.

a) Using the score provided, perform 'Paragraph 7' and record your performance.
b) Did you feel that you had an input into composing this piece?
c) When you were performing, did you alter your ideas to suit what you heard around you?
d) Were you concerned with producing consonant harmonies or did you enjoy the inevitable discords?
e) Did you tune your notes so that they fitted with the other performers or did you deliberately sing slightly out of tune?

Perform the piece again, changing your answers to questions b–e to see what effect the changes have to the piece. Record the second performance.

f) Compare the two recordings. Did the piece sound different when you listened to the recording than when you were performing it?

Experimental approaches to composition for voice

Solo for Voice 22 (1970) by John Cage is written for two performers and electronics. The performers are instructed, quite precisely, how and when to breathe, how long the breaths should be and whether they should breathe through the nose or mouth. The resulting sounds are fed through effects processors and subjected to **reverb**, **flanger**, **delay**, **pan** and other effects to achieve the finished piece.

The performers never produce a sound by the normal means of singing, humming or speaking. In this piece, Cage has focused on exploring the possibilities of breathing as a musical device, excluding all other musical material. Rhythm and timbral exploration are the most important musical elements evident – pitch and harmony are ignored completely.

Cage's *Solo for Voice 49* (1970) is another experimental vocal piece, but the simple three-note melody itself could belong to several other genres. The voice has a piano accompaniment but but not in the way you might expect! The piano lid is closed and the pianist instructed to hit the case in various places to a given rhythm. It is this unconventional use of the piano as an accompaniment to the voice that makes the piece experimental.

Beyond acoustic instruments – the rise of electronics

In the twentieth century, instruments developed as never before. From the earliest experiments with synthesizers at the start of the century to the sophisticated **virtual modelling synthesizers** and **samplers** of today, the developments in music technology have completely changed the way we make and listen to music.

Along the way, composers have adopted some of the emerging electronic devices and discarded others. Olivier Messiaen (1908–92) was one of the first composers to employ an electronic instrument in mainstream music when he used the **Ondes Martenot** in several of his compositions.

Composers such as Stockhausen, Pierre Boulez (b.1925) and Luciano Berio (1925–2003), who were obsessed with controlling every element of their music, were particularly fascinated with electronic sound because they could completely control the sound. They could change the waveform itself (the building block of any sound); they could alter the

Glossary

delay an effect, similar to echo, involving the repetition of a sound at a set time interval for a given number of repeats, with each repeat quieter than the one before

flanger an effect produced by feeding a percentage of a delayed sound source back into the original – the aural effect is a sweeping or 'swooshing' sound

Ondes Martenot an early synthesizer

pan spreading a signal in the stereo field by feeding different levels of the sound to the left and right speakers

reverb the effect produced when a sound is reflected by the surrounding surfaces

samplers devices used to capture and manipulate a sound, often by changing its pitch or by playing selected snippets of the original

virtual modelling synthesizer a software program which acts as a synthesizer, using the processing power of the host computer to copy aspects of another sound source and allow for manipulations of the sound that would not otherwise be physically possible

attack, **decay** and **timbre** of the sound along with all the other elements such as dynamics, **tempo** and so on. These composers all used serialism to control almost every aspect of their music before they began using electronics to take the concept even further. They used electronics in much of their music in the 1950s, collaborating with several large studios to produce their pieces.

Moment form

Stockhausen was one of the major innovators in the genre of electronic music. As his work with the building blocks of sound progressed, he found that it was impossible to organize his music using traditional forms and structures (such as ternary or rondo form). He suggested that in music up until this point the emphasis had been on creating structures that led to musical climaxes at various points, often with phrases marked out with **cadences** and key structures. In electronic music, emphasis is placed on timbre, texture, combinations of timbres and movement in space (panning). In music such as the extract from 'Teil 2' of *Kontakte* (1958–60) (which you will listen to in Task 8), the listener focuses on 'the now'. At any given instant, the music might present a peak or a trough, hence the sense of direction or time is lost. There is no traditional development in pieces of this nature. The piece ends when the material has all been exploited as much as it can be. Stockhausen called this philosophy of structuring his music 'moment form'.

Glossary

attack the part of a sound that occurs immediately after it is sounded. The speed of the attack determines how quickly a note 'speaks': a sound which gradually fades in has a slow attack, but a sound which is very sudden has a fast attack

cadence two chords at the end of a musical phrase. Four main types: perfect, imperfect, interrupted and plagal

decay the last part of a sound; the speed of the decay determines how long it takes for the sound to fade away

tempo speed of the music

timbre particular tone colour of an instrument or voice

8 'Teil 2', of *Kontakte*, Stockhausen   CD1: 19

When listening to this piece, ensure you are positioned between the speakers to fully appreciate the way the sounds move from left to right.

Arrange the following list of musical elements in order of importance for this piece of music: the most important first and the least important last.

- Pitch
- Timbre
- Silence
- Harmony
- Dynamics
- Tempo
- Rhythm
- Texture
- Placement of sounds (left and right)

Many will argue that some works by Cage and Cardew are not 'real music', and as such they were never part of the musical mainstream. But Cage and Cardew have influenced composers who have followed them and have opened up possibilities that would never have been considered without their musical experimentation.

Area of Study 3:

Popular music in context

Popular music is music that is the most widely distributed through the different media channels (radio, television, record sales and so on). This is a purely quantitative idea of popularity – it deals only with the number of items distributed or sold rather than with the quality of the music.

Record companies are the most powerful entities in the music industry. They invest money in bands and artists in the hope that they will make a profit through the sale of CDs, DVDs, ringtones, merchandise, radio airplay and so on. Sometimes the artists in whom they have invested so much money

sell hundreds of thousands of albums, so the record company makes a great deal of money. Other artists may not do so well and fail to repay the initial investment. Few record companies like to take risks, and as such they will do their utmost to ensure that an artist is already popular before they sign them, or that they play in an already 'popular' style.

No one element makes a song or a style popular – it is usually a combination of a strong melody, a good hook line to stick in the memory, a strong beat for dancing to in clubs and being the right sort of music at the right time to appeal to the right people.

Popular artists can be a lucrative investment for record companies.

Other factors determining who the next popular artist or song will be include:

- the amount of radio airplay a new single receives
- the amount of advertising in all areas of the media for a forthcoming album
- critical reviews of forthcoming works
- whether an artist has an established fan base
- how good the video is for the single
- what big names are associated with the music.

Sometimes new and innovative music will become popular due to certain social conditions or other influencing factors that make it possible for many people to be exposed to the music. In the age of digital music distribution, it is becoming increasingly easy for artists to produce their music by themselves without having to sign to a major record label.

In this Area of Study we will look at three areas of popular music in Britain:

- Dance music 1985–present day
- Songs from musicals
- Britpop.

Dance music 1985–present day

In the chapter on dance music we will look at:

- the different genres of dance music
- how the style became so popular.

Club dance songs are judged to be popular by how many times they are played in clubs and how many singles are sold. DJs are the most powerful people in the world of club dance music. If they decide to play a track night after night then the audience will perceive it as being very popular and may well buy the CD, but if a DJ never plays a track then the audience will not hear it and therefore will not buy it. Any track that makes people get out of their seats and move to the dance floor is likely to be played repeatedly by DJs. Lyrics are not important in dance music, but a strong hook line is necessary.

Songs from musicals

In the chapter on songs from musicals we will look at:

- the different musical styles that have been used in musicals
- the most popular composers.

In the world of musical theatre it is vital to fill the theatre from the very first night of a show. Composers of musical theatre will often write in styles that are currently popular or release certain songs from the musicals as singles to act as advertising for the show. Again, advertising and good reviews are absolutely critical to the success of a show, and often the name of the performers will attract an audience rather than the quality of the music itself. Musicals are judged to be popular by how long they run while maintaining high ticket sales for the theatres that stage them.

Britpop and its influences

In the chapter on Britpop we will look at:

- the origins of the Britpop style
- the main bands who were to shape Britpop.

Britpop is an example of a style that arose through a combination of different social conditions. The election of a new Labour government, a rekindling of national identity, the swamping of the British rock music market by American bands and many other conditions set the scene for the emergence of a joyfully British rock genre. As with many genres born out of a certain social climate, Britpop was always going to have a limited time as one of the most popular music styles in the UK, but it did leave its mark on the music industry.

Dance music 1985–present day

In this topic you will learn about:
- the major styles of club dance music
- the role of the DJ
- the roots of club dance music
- how to write a basic dance track.

Performance

The composition tasks for this chapter have been listed as performance and composition tasks. This is because there are few obvious ways to present a performance linked to club dance music other than using the music technology performance option. This allows you to present a sequence as a performance so you can combine the work you do on your dance music composition with the performance. See the chapter on preparing your coursework (starting on page 128) for more details of this option.

What you need to know

Dance music has a very large and fanatical fan base. People love to categorize music, and dance music fans are no exception.

The result is that there are many genres and sub-genres of dance music, with more added every week, with names that change depending on your location (and possibly time of day). There are some clear musical elements that separate the main genres – **tempo** (bpm, or beats per minute), make-up of the rhythm track, **timbres** used and structure. The combination of these different elements is different for each genre.

You do not have to learn to tell the difference between the genres and sub-genres for your GCSE just by listening. One of the reasons for this is that dance music is continually evolving. It is important, however, to have some understanding of what the major genres consist of and how the form known as club dance music evolved.

The table on page 73 provides a brief summary of some of the major club dance music styles.

Glossary

tempo speed of the music

timbre particular tone colour of an instrument or voice

Electronica	Any music that depends mostly on electronic instruments
Dub (early 1970s)	• The earliest known example of '**MCing**' • Based on reggae with vocals removed
Ambient (late 1970s)	• Brian Eno was the father of Ambient • Influenced by minimalism and experimental music • Often uses sounds from the natural environment • Often used as 'chillout' music
Euro synth-based pop (1980s)	The main pop music of the 1980s, common in Europe more so than the USA e.g. Depeche Mode, The Pet Shop Boys, Kraftwerk
Electro (early 1980s)	A mixture of **hip-hop**, **funk** and European synth-based pop
Techno (early 1980s)	• Sometimes used as an umbrella term for lots of dance music genres • Descended from Euro synth-based pop and electro
Balearic beats (1980s)	A form of club dance in Spain in the 1980s where DJs would mix in music from all sorts of cultures to the normal Eurobeat sets
House (mid-1980s)	• First played in 'The Warehouse' club in Chicago (USA) • **4-to-the-floor** bass drum • Influenced by disco, soul, funk and Euro synth-based pop
Garage (deep house) (mid-1980s)	• Influenced by disco and soul • First played in New York's 'Paradise Garage', hence the name
Acid house (late 1980s)	• Uses the Roland TB303 bass synth for bass sounds • Based on house influenced by psychedelia • Was the genre played at the early raves in the late 1980s
Hardhouse (late 1980s)	• Harder-edged sounds than house • House with a sparse texture
Trance (early 1990s)	• Very prominent bass drum beat and hi-hats • Often includes searing **analogue synth** lead sounds and atmosphere sounds • Uses breaks in the same way as progressive house
Jungle (early 1990s)	• Approximately 160 bpm • Influenced by house and hip-hop • Uses **breakbeats** • Was first played in the London club 'Jungle'
Trip-hop (early 1990s)	Downbeat, moody hip-hop
Hardcore/gabba (early 1990s)	• Aggressive, fast techno – gabba is the extreme form of hardcore, known to exceed speeds of 1000 bpm • Uses hard-edged, aggressive sounds
Goa (1990s)	A form of trance music with particular influences from Indian music
Drum 'n' bass (mid-1990s)	• About 160 bpm or above • Uses breakbeats and is a direct descendant of jungle
Speed garage (mid-1990s)	Fusion of garage, jungle and house
Progressive house (mid-1990s)	• A blend of trance and house • Texture gradually builds every eight or sixteen bars, then followed by a break after which the process is repeated

What is club dance music?

Club dance music is simply whatever DJs are playing in clubs.

The most important season for clubbing is the summer. Those 18–30 year-olds who want to go clubbing book their summer holidays in locations such as Ibiza for a fortnight of clubbing, dancing and absolutely not resting and relaxing.

Every summer the biggest clubs compete for the biggest names in the world of DJing, knowing that this will help to draw in bigger crowds and therefore make the club more profit. The DJs themselves have to try to think of new ways of presenting their musical material every year while keeping the dance floor full for as long as the club is open (which may be up to 24 hours a day).

DJs are the centre of dance music. They define the styles. They decide what will be the biggest hits (or **anthems**) of the summer. They keep people coming into the clubs and determine which artists will become the next big thing.

Unlike the music itself, the big name DJs have remained much the same over the last few years, with only a few new names added each year. The biggest names since the late 1990s have included Judge Jules, Tall Paul, Brandon Block, Paul Oakenfold and Fatboy Slim (among many others).

Glossary

4-to-the-floor very prominent, regular bass drum played on each beat of a 4/4 bar

analogue synth synthesizer which uses voltage controlled oscillators, filters and amplifiers in conjunction with envelope generators, low frequency oscillators and other analogue circuitry to create and manipulate waveforms which are heard via a loudspeaker

anthem a song that has achieved a certain longevity due to its popularity and is often instantly recognisable by its distinctive introduction

Well-known DJs can help fill even the largest dance venues.

1 *The Logical Song*, Scooter

Find a copy of *The Logical Song* by Scooter from 2002.

a) List the order in which the parts appear as the track progresses (for example, 1 – drums, 2 – bass and so on). Stop when the MC says 'Good morning'. If you do not know the exact name of a sound, try to describe it (for example, abrasive synth sound).

b) There are several 'breakdowns' in the track when several parts drop out (including the bass drum). What effect does this have on the listener?

c) Are the lyrics simple or complex? Why do you think this is?

What do DJs play?

DJs play many genres of music, chosen to encourage the clubbers to dance. A DJ is employed on the basis of how many clubbers they can draw to the club. Different clubs gain a reputation for specializing in particular genres of music. DJs may specialize in garage, jungle (or drum 'n' bass) or hardcore in addition to the standard anthems of the summer. Most will include some house, techno and progressive house at some point in their sets, and perhaps some disco, soul and funk, depending on the club.

Trance music is by far the most common genre played, with most of the big 'anthems' being trance numbers. Almost all DJs will include at least some elements of trance in their sets. This is because trance has the strong '4-to-the-floor' beat at about 140 bpm that clubbers find most natural to dance to. There is a theory that this is because 140 bpm is the average heart rate of clubbers as they are dancing to the music. Trance can also be known as progressive house. Techno, trance and progressive house have many similar elements and the terms can be used interchangeably.

Glossary

breakbeats drum patterns, often high tempo, which include a significant amount of syncopation and polyrhythms

tempo speed of the music

A sequencing package, with the drum editor window opened.

2 4-to-the-floor

a) Open the sequencing package used in your school (for example, Cubasis, Sonar, Logic or Cubase). You will see the usual opening screen or dialog box.

b) Click on track 10 and check that this is set to MIDI channel 10 (this is the drum track by convention).

c) Open up the drum editor (or piano roll/matrix edit screen). You should see a window similar to the screenshot on page 75 with the drum names listed down the left-hand side of the window. If this does not appear check with your teacher or check the manual for details of how to make these appear.

d) Where a diamond appears alongside an instrument name, it represents a hit of the instrument at the time shown in the timeline at the top of the window. Using the pencil tool, copy the drum pattern given in the screenshot.

e) Play back the loop. Does it sound authentic?

f) The **velocities** (loudness) of the individual hits are normally edited to give accents in appropriate places. For example, if all the hi-hat hits were equally loud, they would form an exceedingly boring loop. Experiment with changing the velocities to hear the effect (the bar graph-like pane at the bottom of the editor can be set to represent velocities that you can then edit with the pencil tool).

g) Make the bass drum hits as loud as possible (velocity = 127).

Club dance music timbres (rhythm section)

When you listen to different club dance tracks, you will notice that the same timbres are used in many of the songs. Dance artists have their favourite **sound modules** (devices that can be linked to a sequencer to produce sound) and synthesizers (synths) that they use most frequently to produce their tracks. This collection of electronic noise production devices will always include at least one analogue synth. The drum track itself is either produced electronically from the likes of a Roland TR909 (or a machine made to sound like the Roland TR909) or from a selection of electronically manipulated samples. This is one of the reasons why your drum loop in Task 2 does not sound completely authentic. Try selecting the electronic drum kit from the list available (instead of the standard drum kit) and you will hear an instant improvement.

Glossary

velocities a piece of information included in a MIDI note which translates as the loudness of the note

sound modules devices that convert MIDI information into audio that can be played through loudspeakers

The analogue synth is almost always the source of the next most important timbre in club dance – the bass. The Roland TB303 was the original source of the bass sounds for acid house, but other genres use other sound sources such as the Novation Bass Station or Novation Supernova. Drum 'n' bass obviously gives a great deal of emphasis to the bass, and artists in this genre will spend a long time trying out many pieces of equipment to find just the right bass sound with lots of power behind it.

3 *Pump up the Jam*, Technotronic   CD2: 1

Technotronic were one of the main bands behind the sub-genre Eurobeat. This was a European form of house music, heavily influenced by Euro synth-based pop. The song *Pump up the Jam* was released in 1989 and is considered a dance floor classic.

Listen to *Pump up the Jam* by Technotronic.

a) What is the structure of the song? There is a bass drum hit on every beat (except where it stops playing) and the phrases are generally four or eight bars long. Use the words 'intro', 'verse', 'chorus', 'instrumental' and 'break' to describe the sections and make a note of how many bars each section lasts for. Do not include the fade at the end of the song.

b) Are the timbres electronic or acoustic?

The development of club dance music

Pump up the Jam is considered a classic because it is one of the earlier examples of club dance music that is still played today. It might seem odd to think of a song that is less than twenty years old as a classic, but the world of dance music moves as fast as the technology used to make it, so major developments happen very quickly and music consequently sounds quite dated.

The table on page 73 sets out the major genres in dance music, the dates they were developed and some identifying features of each genre. The 'family tree' on page 78 shows how the genres are all interlinked in some way and the roots of the style as a whole.

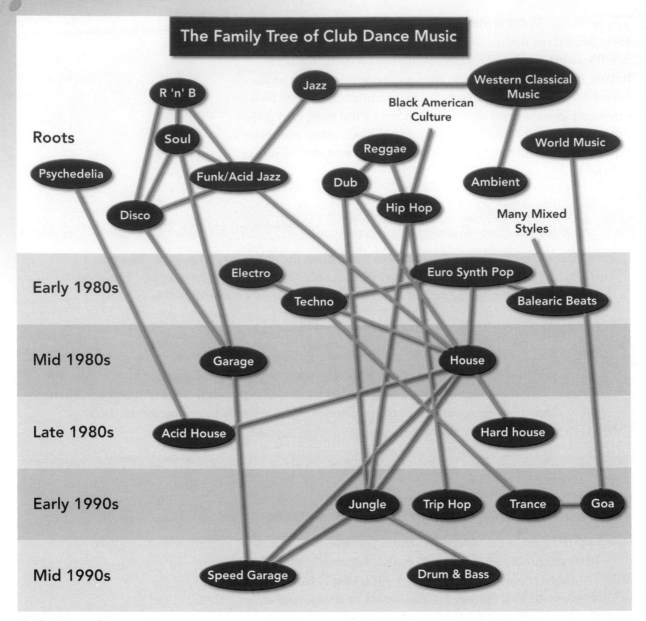

The family tree of dance music.

Roots of club dance music

Funk, disco, jazz, R'n'B (rhythm and blues), reggae, Western classical music and psychedelia are just some of the styles that have fed into dance music as we know it. Music from around the world has also played its part, but the effect will depend on what part of the world the dance music itself is from (as you might expect). Some genres are defined by the type of world music they contain – for example, goa is a blend of trance and Indian music.

Dub

The art of taking an original song and 'remixing' it can be traced back to the late 1960s when Bob Marley's producer, King Tubby, took some reggae tracks, removed the vocal part and overdubbed some effects (hence 'dub') on the instrumental tracks. The style developed in the early 1970s when King Tubby and Lee Perry (among others) turned it into a marketing ploy. They would record the instrumentalists and vocalists in one session and release the song as a single, but on the B-side they would put a dub remix of the track, displaying their own creativity as well as saving money on recording costs.

These dub artists can be considered to be the first DJs; they were employed in the mid-1950s (before dub was developed) to use their 'sound systems' to play music through. These were basically PA systems through which they were able to amplify their music. They became popular because they were cheaper to hire than a band of musicians. They would often sign artists to record exclusively for them so that they had an edge in the market by playing exclusive tracks on their sound systems.

Chicago house

In Chicago, in the mid-1980s, DJs such as Frankie Knuckles and Farley 'Jackmaster' Funk pioneered a sound that was to become known as house (named after the club where it was first played – The Warehouse). The DJs would take existing tracks and remix them, or cut them up, mixing them together with other tracks because they did not have enough new material to play. Frankie Knuckles is sometimes known as 'the godfather of house' because he was the first to bring some of these ideas to the Chicago clubs.

Music played in The Warehouse ranged from disco and soul through to Euro synth-based pop. Sometimes the DJs would bring in a drum machine to exaggerate the '4-to-the-floor' bass drum beat that was characteristic of house music.

The track *Pump up the Volume* by M/A/R/R/S (1987), which you will listen to in Task 4, is a typical example of the sparse feel of house music when it became popular in the UK in 1986–7.

4 *Pump up the Volume*, M/A/R/R/S

CD2: 2

Listen to *Pump up the Volume* by M/A/R/R/S.

a) Write down all the lyrics you can hear.
b) What sounds are there in the track apart from the percussion/drums, the bass and the vocals?

c) Describe the texture of the music. How does it change (if at all) as the track progresses?

Acid house

The first acid house track was called *Acid Tracks* and was released in 1987 by Phuture. The style is characterized by the sound of the Roland TB303 – a small synth released originally to create the bass sounds required to go along with Roland's drum machines that were already popular. It was a very cheap device that soon fell out of use after its original release, but with the advent of acid house it became the machine for all DJs and producers to own. The default sound could only be described as an 'acid' sound because of its abrasive, squelchy nature – hence the name of the track and the name of the style.

Although there were other drug-related connotations to the name, acid house artists worked hard to distance themselves from links with the hallucinogenic drug LSD.

Acid house was the style that became very popular in the UK and led to the start of the UK rave scene in the late 1980s.

New York garage

While the popularity of Chicago house music was gradually dying down, another scene was starting in New York.

In a club called the Paradise Garage, the DJ Larry Levan pioneered a style that was much more melodic than house, taking its influences more from soul and R'n'B. This style again took its name from the club where it was first played, becoming known as garage. In the UK, the Ministry of Sound, based in London, was heavily influenced by the garage sound.

5 Add a little bass

a) Write a simple chord sequence using no more than four chords. It should be repetitive and last either two or four bars. The chords should be basic **triads** – it sometimes works best if they are all **major** chords.

b) Write a bass line. This should complement both the drum track (which you have already written in Task 2) and the chord sequence. It may be a simple root note idea, repeating the root note of the chord over and over in quavers, or on offbeat quavers or it may be a slightly more complicated riff, based on the chords.

c) Find a suitable timbre for your bass track and record it onto your sequencer.

d) Add the chord sequence using an appropriate synth sound. You should not simply play one chord per bar but should add interest by playing each chord using a set rhythm.

e) Write a vocal hook. This should be very simple (use *Pump up the Volume*, which you heard in Task 4, as a guide). A vocal hook consists of one snappy phrase that does not necessarily have to make sense – it just has to have a good rhythm and make an impact on the listener.

f) If you have the facility on your sequencer to record your vocal track, then you should record it on top of the other tracks and experiment with it by chopping it up into small bits and pasting lots of these bits together to get the 'stutter' technique. For example, if your vocal hook was 'Dance to the beat', you could record it and then chop it into small bits, as shown above:

Dance to the beat	To the beat
Da	Be
Dance	Beat
Dance to the	

g) The syllables 'da' and 'be' should be copied and pasted in very close succession to give the stutter effect – 'da-da-da-da-da-da-da-da-dance'. If your sequencer does not have the ability to record audio, you can experiment with doing the same thing in a live performance. This will be much more difficult, but you might come up with some clever new ideas in the process!

h) You will need to add other sound effects such as those you heard in *Pump up the Volume* if your track is to sound authentic. They should be used to emphasize structural points (such as once every sixteen bars or to highlight the return of a section) rather than being used continuously.

i) Using the structure you worked out from Task 3 as a guide, create a structure for your track. You should include a build-up where the parts are introduced one by one, a breakdown to just drums (or drums and vocals) and a section where you introduce new material to keep the listener's interest. Listen to several club dance tracks to get ideas for structuring your track as well as listening to how others have incorporated sound effects into their tracks and what timbres they have used.

M25 rave scene

In the late 1980s, clubs in London all had restrictions on how long they were able to stay open at night, but clubbers often wanted to keep on dancing, even after the club had closed. This demand encouraged people to find alternative venues to stage more parties after closing time. The extra parties were illegal, and after the police started to evict clubbers from the established venues, the organizers were gradually forced to stage them further and further from the centre of London. By the summer of 1988, mass parties were organized at various venues around the fringes of London, generally in large warehouses and abandoned hangers around the M25 motorway.

These parties attracted a criminal element and a lot of drug dealing, especially in the drug Ecstasy. They also attracted a lot of police attention and so moved venue from night to night in an effort to avoid detection.

The music played at these raves was centred around acid house, and often many DJs would play short sets over the course of the night. The DJs would play the most popular tracks they had to get the dance floor as full as possible for their set – giving rise to summer anthems.

The rave scene faded out as the authorities gradually devoted more resources to breaking up the different parties that were organized.

Madchester

In 1989, clubs such as the Haçienda and Thunderdome in Manchester became extremely popular with clubbers around the north of England and the Midlands. These clubs were licensed to open until 2am, but clubbers would still seek other venues after they closed. The emergence of the party atmosphere in Manchester at the end of the 1980s became known as the 'Madchester' scene. The music played in these clubs was primarily house and acid house.

This scene helped to create the indie-dance crossover style of Happy Mondays and The Stone Roses (see pages 97–98 for more details).

Glossary

major western tonal music in bright sounding keys. A major key has four semitones between the first and third notes

triads a three note chord ('Tri' means three)

The 1990s onwards

In the 1990s, many new genres of club dance music sprang up around the UK, categorized by tempo, timbre, type of beat, structure and so on. The table on page 73 summarizes these, and the 'family tree' on page 78 shows how they are all inter-related. Each genre has its own social context and particular group of devotees. Genres such as house, garage and acid house are the most important for setting the scene of club dance culture in the UK before it diversified into its many different elements.

6 *Somebody to Love*, Jefferson Airplane and *Somebody to Love*, Boogie Pimps (Salt Shaker remix) CD2: 3 & 4

Listen first to Jefferson Airplane's version of *Somebody to Love* (1967), then to the Boogie Pimps version (2003).

a) How is the original track used in the remix? Is it used in its entirety, only snippets or both?

b) Does the remix use the same chord pattern as the original or has it changed?

c) Does the remix use only music from the original or does it include new music of its own?

Remixing

The art of remixing is widespread in the world of dance music. Almost all tracks are remixed to some extent, either by the original producer searching for the best way a track can be presented to the record-buying public or by another artist using the material in a different way. Even rock bands and other artists without any connections to the world of dance music will pay a producer to do a remix of one of their songs to make it suitable for use in clubs or for a B-side.

In recent years, there has been an increase in the number of tracks in the charts that are remixes of songs by other artists, or even classical composers. In many ways, these can be just like cover versions of the song, with the new artist attempting a different approach to the track, but sometimes they can include parts of the original track. There have been cases where the original artist has sued the remix artist for use of the original track without consent – a famous case was when Vanilla Ice used the bass line from Queen's *Under Pressure* in his 1990 hit *Ice Ice Baby*. Any material can be remixed for personal enjoyment without fear of reprisal, but if you intend to sell your work, you must seek copyright clearance from the owner of the original material.

Songs from musicals

In this topic you will learn about:
- the origins of the musical
- different types of musical
- how to write a song for a musical.

The world of musical theatre has a history as rich and varied as any other area of music. It takes its influences from a wide variety of sources, including the popular music of the day, opera, Western Classical music, jazz, rock and many more, depending on the type of musical and its target audience.

There are a huge range of musicals that the music lover can choose to see on any night of the year. Some musicals have achieved the status of classics, having run for many years without interruption in the most important centres of musical theatre – Broadway (New York) and the West End (of London). In other cases, shows that are available to see this week may no longer be running next week because they are not profitable enough. Such is the nature of musical theatre – it is a populist genre, with shows surviving only because enough people want to come and see them night after night. It is important, therefore, that the composer of a musical gets the balance right between writing songs that will appeal to a large audience and delivering a spectacle that will encourage people to come and see it.

A scene from Starlight Express, *depicting the spectacle that musical theatre aims to deliver.*

The origins of the musical

Musical theatre has been present at least since the time of Ancient Greece. In the last few centuries it has gradually evolved from many different styles of entertainment, both musical and non-musical.

The development of musicals as we now know them had different paths in Europe and the United States of America, catering for different audiences and tastes. Originally, American musical theatre borrowed heavily from Europe, importing all the popular new music, but this trend was reversed after the First World War when Europe (Britain in particular) began to import the American musicals almost to the point of excluding home-grown shows from all the theatres. With the sudden arrival of Andrew Lloyd Webber and Tim Rice onto the scene in 1970, British musicals became popular once again.

Vaudeville and burlesque

A form of musical entertainment popular in the 1700s, **vaudeville** was essentially a set of 'borrowed' popular songs with new words set to them. The lyrical content tended to be quite rude, designed to shock and entertain. An example of this style is *The Beggar's Opera* by John Gay (1685–1732), popular in Europe in 1728, dealing with subject matter such as prostitutes, thieves and their antics.

Burlesque was a little more Classical in its style, often a parody of other serious plays and musical works. By the mid-1800s, burlesque tended to include an element of striptease.

Opéra-bouffe and operetta

Opéra-bouffe was at its most popular from about 1870 up until the First World War, and many are still performed today. It consisted of music especially composed for the theatre (rather than taken from existing popular songs), with words set to the music. The music would be in a style suitable for light opera, but not for the more serious, high-art kind of opera.

One of the most famous examples of opéra-bouffe is *Orpheus in the Underworld* (1858) by Jacques Offenbach (1819–80) – a slightly comical take on the legend of Orpheus and Eurydice. The famous 'Can-can' comes from this piece, when Eurydice is sent back to the underworld to dance with the others consigned to a fate with Pluto (highlighting the comical nature of the work).

Glossary

burlesque a parody or humorous piece

opéra-bouffe a light opera, often with spoken dialogue and some comical content

vaudeville a form of entertainment, popular in the 1700s, in which popular songs were performed with alternative words

Perhaps the most famous of English composers in this style were the pair William Gilbert (1836–1911), the lyricist, and Arthur Sullivan (1842–1900), the composer, writing such famous works as *H.M.S. Pinafore* (1878), *The Pirates of Penzance* (1879) and *The Mikado* (1885). Gilbert and Sullivan's works combined the humour of the burlesque with a particularly English type of light Classical music – a winning combination for lasting popularity in England.

Operetta is, as its name suggests, like a little light opera. It was full of nineteenth-century romanticism and nostalgia, often referring to a made-up central European country called Ruritania, involving the romantic mishaps of dukes, duchesses, lords and ladies. There is a significant crossover between the opéra-bouffe and operetta styles, with operetta often seen as a development of opéra-bouffe.

Importantly, although these styles originated in Europe, they became very popular in America in the late 1800s, especially the works of Gilbert and Sullivan.

Early musical theatre in America

In addition to the musicals imported from Europe, the USA had its own forms of musical theatre. These were all to influence the development of the early twentieth-century American musical.

Extravaganzas were a form of entertainment very similar to the Saturday night variety shows of the 1980s and 90s. They included all forms of entertainment from singing and dancing through to magicians and so on. They were popular in the USA from the 1860s through to 1900.

Minstrelsy was a form of entertainment popular in the second half of the 1800s. It consisted of white people made up in 'black-face' to imitate black people in a general parody and exaggeration of any character traits. It also poked fun at the rich and powerful. This style was popular before the emergence of civil rights movements or any concept of political correctness.

Melodramas, popular around the same time as minstrelsy, were plays that included some musical cues for different scenes. They were largely driven by dialogue (as opposed to songs) but were important because they made use of music in a stage play.

Glossary

operetta light opera

Glossary

extravaganzas stage shows containing a variety of acts

melodramas dramas in which spoken lines are punctuated by music

minstrelsy form of entertainment, popular in the 1800s, in which white actors would be made up in 'blackface' to imitate black slaves and poke fun at the rich and powerful

The libretto

The libretto is the story of the musical arranged into a form that can be sung. More specifically, the libretto is the actual text and words of an opera or musical. It is vital to the success of a musical that the libretto be suitable for the target audience – it needs to be witty, poignant, comical, serious and include references to current issues, all in the appropriate places. It was not until the early 1900s that the libretto started taking on a much more important role, linking all the different numbers that made up the show with a common theme. By the 1920s, the Americans really cracked the combination of libretto and music, incorporating much more risqué themes with all the influences listed above and the new American popular music – jazz.

1930–60

The British musical was stuck in a rut during this time. Censorship stopped the composer and librettist from making any reference to the monarchy or any living person. Overt references to sex were also frowned upon but not expressly forbidden. American composers of this time worked in much more liberal conditions. When the American shows finally did come to the West End after the First World War, they had a tremendous impact. During this era, the most important composers were American – Rodgers and Hammerstein (*Oklahoma!* (1943), *Carousel* (1945)), Irving Berlin (*Annie Get Your Gun* (1946)) and Cole Porter (*Anything Goes* (1934), *Kiss Me, Kate* (1948)).

1 'Anything Goes', Cole Porter

CD 2: 5

Listen to 'Anything Goes' by Cole Porter.

a) How has this song been influenced by jazz?
b) The accompaniment for the first section of the song (up to 'Plymouth Rock would land on them') is very different from the accompaniment for the rest of the song. How does this emphasize the lyrics?

It was not until the 1960s that the show *Oliver* (by Lionel Bart) revived the fortunes of the British musical. It turned out to be the longest running British show on a Broadway stage at the time.

Andrew Lloyd Webber and Tim Rice

While Bart's *Oliver* went some way to reviving the British musical, what really changed the face of musical theatre in Britain was the release of *Jesus Christ Superstar* (1970) written by Tim Rice (lyrics) and Andrew Lloyd Webber (music).

Jesus Christ Superstar caused a stir for several reasons. It was controversial in its choice of theme (the life of Jesus seen through the eyes of Judas, who later betrayed him for what he felt to be the greater good); it was sung-through (all the text was sung, with none spoken); and it eventually became a large-scale visual extravaganza.

Jesus Christ Superstar was also first marketed as a concept album rather than being staged. The success of the album merited the staging of the show, marking the beginning of a fabulously successful career for Lloyd Webber and Rice.

The pair followed this up with *Evita* (1978) – again, controversial because the politics were considered very liberal for the time (it tells the story of Eva Peron, an Argentine heroine). The show was one of the most successful ever to hit the West End.

Further successes followed with *Cats* (1981), *Starlight Express* (1984), *Phantom of the Opera* (1986) and many more. Lloyd Webber/Rice musicals came to dominate the stages of the West End, turning around the fortunes of some of the theatres that had been struggling financially and altering the balance of Broadway dominance of the London stage.

Lloyd Webber had a knack of creating extremely singable songs within a package that could be turned into a real spectacle. *Starlight Express* is an example of the extremes to which he would go by turning the whole of the theatre into a series of platforms for the roller-skate-wearing cast to move around.

2 'All I Ask of You', *Phantom of the Opera*, Andrew Lloyd Webber and Tim Rice

CD2: 6

Listen to 'All I Ask of You' while following the piano score below.

No more talk of dark - ness, for - get these wide - eyed fears: I'm

here, noth-ing can harm you, my words will warm and calm you. Let me be your free - dom, let

day-light dry your tears: I'm here, with you, be-side you, to guard you and to guide you.

Say you love me ev - ery wak - ing mo - ment, turn my head with talk of

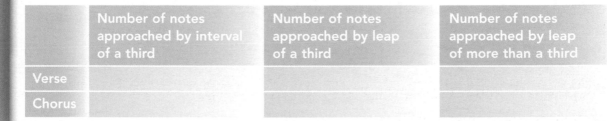

ALL I ASK OF YOU from THE PHANTOM OF THE OPERA
Music:- Andrew Lloyd Webber; Lyrics:- Charles Hart; Additional lyrics:- Richard Stilgoe
© copyright 1986 & 1995 Andrew Lloyd Webber assigned to The Really Useful Group Ltd.
This arrangement © copyright 2001 The Really Useful Group Ltd.
All Rights Reserved. International Copyright Secured.

a) What is the largest melodic interval used in the verse?
b) What is the largest melodic interval used in the chorus?
c) Complete a copy of the following table:

	Number of notes approached by interval of a third	Number of notes approached by leap of a third	Number of notes approached by leap of more than a third
Verse			
Chorus			

Rock operas

Jesus Christ Superstar was one of the first 'rock operas', although it was actually preceded by several shows, including *Hair* (1967), which took the USA by storm. *Hair* included swearing, references to drugs, youth culture and homosexuality, which had been unheard of in a musical before. It also had a considerably more raucous score than other musicals of the time.

The term 'rock opera' (or rock musical) refers to the setting of the text to music, which has more in common with pop and rock music than with Western Classical traditions.

Other important 'rock musicals' include *Tommy* (1969) by The Who (a British rock band popular in the 1960s and 70s), with the hit track 'Pinball Wizard', *Grease* (1978) and *Rent* (1996). *Rent*, like *Hair*, was intended to push the boundaries of acceptability and included issues of sexuality, drug abuse, youth culture and rebellion, with a soundtrack to match. *Little Shop of Horrors* (1986) is another stage production that has since been remade (and given a Hollywood ending) as a film. *The Rocky Horror Picture Show* (1973) is a British musical by Richard O'Brien with a transvestite as its hero, again supported by rock songs throughout.

A scene from the 2002 rock opera We Will Rock You.

Later versions of the 'rock musical' include the looser, collection-of-hit-song style shows that celebrate the work of major bands. These include *Mamma Mia* (1999), celebrating the work of Abba, and *We Will Rock You* (2002), celebrating the work of Queen. Neither of these shows has as structured a libretto as works by the likes of Rice and Webber. Instead, they concentrate on the inclusion of some of the major hits of the artists in question.

3 'One Song Glory', *Rent*, Jonathan Larson

CD2: 7

Listen to 'One Song Glory' by Jonathan Larson.

a) Describe how the instrumentation in 'One Song Glory' is different from the instrumentation in 'All I Ask of You' (from Task 2).

b) Write out the structure of this song using words such as 'verse', 'chorus' and so on rather than letter names.

c) The lyrics are set differently in the verse and the chorus. Describe how the setting of the lyrics differs between the verse and the chorus.

d) Why do you think the composer does this?

Disney shows and shows adapted from the screen

The Lion King (1997), written by Elton John and Tim Rice, has had a very successful transition from the screen to the stage. It has run in the West End since 1999 and is still running at the time of writing. The music introduces an African flavour to the stage along with the Elton John hits from the original film (padded out with some additional, specially written numbers).

The introduction of music from other cultures has been very successful in musicals (notably with the Latin feel introduced into *West Side Story* (1957) by Leonard Bernstein) and may be a contributory factor in *The Lion King*'s success. The songs themselves can also contribute to the musical's popularity. The main track in *The Lion King*, 'Circle of Life', was a major success in the mainstream charts on its release, so it is likely to draw people in to see the show.

Other Disney classics have been adapted for the stage, for example *Beauty and the Beast* (1994) and *The Hunchback of Notre Dame* (1996), but few have matched *The Lion King* so far in popularity.

In the past, shows have often made their way onto the big screen after a successful run in the theatre (for example, *The Sound of Music* (1959), *West Side Story* and *Oliver*), but there is an increasing trend for successful films to be adapted for the stage (such as the Disney classics and *Saturday Night Fever* (1997)).

In general, shows that have been adapted for the stage from successful films have been less successful than the transition in the opposite direction (generally because the glitz of Hollywood does not transfer so well to the stage), but these adaptations are becoming more popular.

Sondheim and Schonberg

There is not enough space to mention all the major composers of musical theatre, but Stephen Sondheim and Claude-Michel Schonberg are composers who made a major contribution to the world of the musical.

Steven Sondheim was originally a lyricist who took on the additional role of composing the music in later years. After his hit *A Little Night Music* (1973), he deliberately started writing shows he knew would be much less commercially acceptable for a while. He wanted to explore a more personal path instead of being a slave to the commercial aspects of writing musicals. *Sweeney Todd* (1979) was a brief departure from this uncommercial path.

Claude-Michel Schonberg composed the music for the world-renowned show *Les Miserables* (1980) with Alain Boublil providing the libretto adapted from Victor Hugo's novel. This was originally a light, short work, but was later remade into the full-scale opus that is now very famous. It outlines life in early to mid 19th century France, including a famous scene where revolutionary students build and man barricades only to be killed by the soldiers. The historical drama is given a human feel by introducing several characters, including the hero (Jean Valjean), love interests and the likeable rogues. The combination of characterization, fine songwriting and scoring, and the weight of the tale, has made this one of the biggest blockbusters in the history of musical theatre.

Writing a song for GCSE Music

For the purposes of GCSE Music, you have to relate your compositions to topics studied. If you are writing a song to relate to this topic, you should try to follow these guidelines.

a) You should have a plot for your musical. Your song should take one aspect of this plot and expand on it from the point of view of one of your characters.

b) The song should contain 'characterization' – it should somehow reveal the personality of the character.

c) You do not need to write the lyrics yourself. A good idea is to adapt lyrics from a novel, a story or a poem that you have enjoyed reading. It is generally a bad idea to try to re-set lyrics that have already been used in a song – you will inevitably start using aspects of the original rhythms and melodies.

d) You should be careful with the setting of your words to ensure that, when they are sung, the rhythms are not clumsy. To do this, sing or speak the words through to your set rhythms. If there is an emphasis on syllables that feels unnatural, then you need to change your rhythm.

e) You might involve some word painting, preferably in a subtle way. An example of **word painting** would be to set the word 'high' as the highest pitched note in a phrase. However, too much of this sounds amateurish. A subtle form of this technique is to set the mood of a song to reflect the mood of the lyrics or, if the mood changes from phrase to phrase, you might alter the mood of the accompaniment and melody to suit it.

f) Think carefully about the structure of your song. Is there a sense of the song building up to a climax? A key change moving into a new section can really help to lift a song. If you use a standard form such as intro-verse-chorus-verse-chorus-middle 8-chorus-chorus-outro, then you should ensure that the middle 8 section contains enough fresh material to maintain interest without straying too far from the feel of the piece as a whole. Some sets of lyrics will not lend themselves to such a structure and will need a very original approach. Consider this carefully when you are choosing your lyrics.

g) Think about the range of the melody itself. If you are writing for an individual, you should consider their vocal range and write to suit.

h) What would be suitable instrumentation for your accompaniment? Do you require soft sounds or harsher sounds, acoustic or electronic? Should they have a strong rhythm or a free-flowing feel? Will they intertwine with the melody, imitate it or simply provide chordal accompaniment? Can you use some of the melodic ideas in your accompaniment?

i) Should the texture stay the same throughout the piece? Allowing the music to 'breathe' where necessary is the mark of a mature composer.

j) You do not actually have to write a song from a musical if you undertake a composing task based on this topic. If you write an instrumental piece, you must show how it links to the topic by, for example, explaining how it forms an interlude between two scenes or how it introduces themes used by the main characters and so on. You should explain these details in your 'Understanding the brief' pro forma.

Glossary

word painting describing word in musical terms. For example, 'rising' would be set to a series of ascending notes, or 'grief' by falling phrases

Britpop and its influences

In this topic you will learn about:
- the context of the Britpop explosion
- the bands who influenced Britpop
- how to write a song in a Britpop style.

The term 'Britpop' could be applied to any popular music written in the British Isles, or even music written for the British market. For the purposes of Edexcel GCSE Music, Britpop itself is much more focused; it consists of the music of Oasis, Blur, Pulp and Suede. These four bands probably have the biggest fan base of all the Britpop bands of the 1990s, but there were many others. Bands such as The Verve, Cast, Supergrass, Elastica and so on were also part of the Britpop scene. This chapter also focuses on the bands who most influenced Britpop.

Indie music

In the early 1980s, political idealism and music came together in the form of **indie music**. The idea came about partly as a rebellion against the dominance of the record industry by major labels and the bands signed to them. Geoff Travis, a Cambridge graduate, set up a music shop in London dedicated to selling records produced by local bands. This idea became very popular, but it lacked the nationwide distribution of the major labels, so he entered into an agreement with many like-minded stores around the country so that they could share the music with each other, taking the bands from being a local act to being heard all around the UK.

Travis's record shop gradually turned into a record label as he took more and more bands under his wing. His label was independent of the major labels, having set up a unique system to distribute the records, hence the term 'indie music' came about.

The concept of Travis's system was that the music itself was of absolute importance – he was not at all interested in making vast profits from others' work. As such, he and his associates would negotiate deals with the bands that allowed them to keep ownership of their own material (major labels claim ownership of the copyright of material recorded by their artists), shared the costs and profits on a largely 50/50 basis and allowed the artists to leave the label when they chose.

Glossary

indie music music distributed by means other than the large record and distribution companies. The smaller record labels who use alternative distribution methods are known as 'independent labels' and artists who record with these labels are known as 'independent' or 'indie' artists

95

The artists themselves shared this philosophy (at least, up to the point when they started attracting major label attention!) and, for a while, it all worked very well and sparked a major upheaval in the way the music industry worked.

In Manchester, Tony Wilson had formed a record label called Factory Records with the sole purpose of funding the first album by Joy Division (called *Unknown Pleasures* (1979)). They used Travis's distribution system to bring the music to the attention of the British public, and it worked very well.

The Smiths

The Smiths, fronted by Morrissey, were probably the most important indie band to come out of the 1980s. All four major Britpop bands list The Smiths as a major influence. They were all that was important about indie music of the time – they were very anti Margaret Thatcher, the Conservative leader, supported the coal miner strikes of the 1980s, were proud of their Englishness, despised major labels (again, until the point they signed to EMI) and avoided the traditional long hair, spandex and make-up of 1980s pop music, choosing a certain soulful scruffiness instead.

Morrissey, frontman of the Smiths.

The Smiths were formed in 1982, their name a reaction against the pretentious names chosen by other bands of the decade. Johnny Marr (guitar) and Morrissey (vocals) married chiming, atmospheric guitar with clever, angst-ridden, self-absorbed lyrics. Morrissey's lyrics often struck a chord with those who also felt angst-ridden or as if life had dealt them an unfair hand. The following example is from *I Know It's Over* taken from the album *The Queen is Dead* (1986).

'Cause tonight is just like any other night
That's why you're on your own tonight
With your triumphs and your charms
While they're in each other's arms...
It's so easy to laugh
It's so easy to hate
It takes strength to be gentle and kind
Over, over, over, over
It's so easy to laugh

It's so easy to hate
It takes guts to be gentle and kind
Over, over
Love is natural and real
But not for you, my love
Not tonight, my love
Love is natural and real
But not for such as you and I, my love.

1 *Hand in Glove*, The Smiths

Listen to the song *Hand in Glove* by The Smiths, taken from the 1984 album *The Smiths*.

a) Describe the vocal style.
b) Study the lyrics below and describe how the music has been set to the words.

Hand in glove
The sun shines out of our behinds
No, it's not like any other love
This one is different – because it's us

Hand in glove
We can go wherever we please
And everything depends upon
How near you stand to me

And if the people stare
Then the people stare
Oh, I really don't know and I really don't care

Kiss my shades...oh...

Hand in glove
The good people laugh
Yes, we may be hidden by rags
But we've something they'll never have

Hand in glove
The sun shines out of our behinds
Yes, we may be hidden by rags
But we've something they'll never have

And if the people stare
Then the people stare
Oh, I really don't know and I really don't care

Kiss my shades...oh...

So, hand in glove I stake my claim
I'll fight to the last breath

If they dare touch a hair on your head
I'll fight to the last breath

For the good life is out there somewhere
So stay on my arm, you little charmer

But I know my luck too well
Yes, I know my luck too well
And I'll probably never see you again
I'll probably never see you again
I'll probably never see you again
Oh...

Madchester

In the late 1980s, the rave culture hit the UK with the advent of acid house (see pages 74–80 on club dance music for more details of the origins of house music). Manchester was an important centre for raves with its Haçienda Club becoming the important club in the north. Members of the bands Happy Mondays and The Stone Roses frequented raves there, soaking up elements of the rave culture.

They incorporated elements of dance music into the indie music they enjoyed, forming a more commercial style altogether. The two bands did not have any of the indie sensitivities about being commercially successful.

Happy Mondays' first EP (extended play record, or half-length album) was called *The Madchester Rave On EP*, coining the phrase 'Madchester' to describe the scene in Manchester at the time. The result was that a generally rundown, industrial city was fast becoming one of the most up and coming cities in the country and a hotspot for new musical talent.

The vocalists for both bands had a similar vocal style, floating over the guitar riffs and additional electronic effects. Both had a somewhat 'nasal' sound, sliding up and down from the notes so that the vocal melody strongly depends on the delivery. Both were proud of their Mancunian accents, so they avoided the affected American accent of other British vocalists.

2 *Step On*, Happy Mondays

CD2: 9

Listen to *Step On* by Happy Mondays (1990).

a) What elements of dance music are present in this song?

b) How successful is the integration of the dance piano riff into the guitar-based music? Give reasons for your answer.

Reactions to American dominance of music

American bands dominated rock music in the early 1990s. In Seattle, a band called Nirvana almost single-handedly made **grunge** the sound that many others tried to imitate. Nirvana's music was technically very straightforward – the lead singer and guitarist, Kurt Cobain, was not a gifted guitarist – but they possessed an energy and drive that made the music very powerful. All around the USA and Britain, guitarists could be heard copying their biggest selling tracks (*Smells Like Teen Spirit* and *Come As You Are* (both 1991)), and because they were so straightforward, it did not take long to learn the tracks and make them sound very convincing.

Home-grown British rock music tended to be quite complex, still reminiscent of the overproduced sounds of the 1980s (a producer would add lots of extra parts and sounds to a record, making it sound interesting, but almost impossible for budding musicians to recreate), or it was heavily influenced by dance music, so it often failed to appeal to fans of guitar-driven music. It was this background that helped to inspire a wave of musical patriotism in the mid-1990s now called Britpop.

Glossary

grunge genre of rock music from the North West of the USA inspired by indie music, punk and thrash metal and at its most popular during the late 1980s and early 1990s

Blur

In March 1990, a band signed to Food Records and immediately changed their name from Seymour to Blur. They wrote music that was obviously inspired by the British bands of the 1980s, but they included elements of their own that came from the musical upbringing of their frontman and singer, Damon Albarn. He had been brought up in a household where Classical art and music were held in high esteem, so he felt it was natural to try to bring some elements of this into pop music. He felt it was important to experiment, adding unexpected twists to his songs. This experimentation can be heard in the track for Task 3, *Parklife*.

From 1991–3, Blur had an intense rivalry with another Britpop band, Suede. To start with, it seemed as if Suede would win this 'battle of the bands' but in 1993, with the release of their album *Modern Life is Rubbish*, Blur started to make an impact. It was not until 1994, however, and their more famous 'battle of the bands' with Oasis that Blur were really able to capture the attention of the record-buying public.

Oasis had just achieved a great deal of success with their debut album *Definitely Maybe* (1994). They were a band who gloried in their Englishness, flying the flag for British music in the wake of the grunge invasion of the early 1990s. The press latched on to the patriotic tendencies of both bands and proclaimed a 'battle of the bands' when the two bands had singles and albums in the charts at the same time. The publicity did both bands a great deal of good, raising the profiles of both.

With their album *Parklife* (1994), Blur achieved critical acclaim. The single of the same name is a commentary on life away from the 9 to 5 grind that traps so many people. It is a good example of how Britpop artists write songs about the everyday, often with a unique viewpoint, and also how they are proud of their regional accents (in this case cockney).

3 *Parklife*, Blur

Find a copy of the song *Parklife* by Blur.

a) What sounds in the intro give this song the sense of being about everyday events?

b) How many chords are used in the verse?

c) How does the song build up in the chorus?

d) What elements of the song make it sound 'British'?

Suede

Britpop was a small world and involved a limited number of people, so there was often some connection between members of rival bands. In the case of Suede and Blur, this consisted of a rivalry over a girl. When Justine Frischmann left Brett Anderson (the lead singer of Suede) for Damon Albarn, this gave Suede the impetus to really kick-start their musical career. The personal trauma gave Anderson a much darker view of life than he'd had before and helped him bond with his guitarist, Bernard Butler, both as friends and musicians. They viewed themselves as the new Johnny Marr and Morrissey (the driving force behind The Smiths). In early 1992, they signed to an indie label (Nude Records) and released two singles that received critical acclaim.

Suede, with Brett Anderson on the far left.

Suede's lyrics are often risqué or dark, reflecting Anderson's state of mind at the time he wrote the songs. This was reflected in Butler's often quite aggressive guitar playing. Anderson was also very keen to preserve his accent while singing rather than adopting an American accent.

Pulp

Through the 1980s, a young Jarvis Cocker from Sheffield gradually honed his skills as a songwriter and bandleader by going through many incarnations of his band Pulp. They had early success with recognition on John Peel's radio programme and a single released in 1990, but they were not signed to a label to record an album until 1993. By this time, they had refined their bittersweet style to perfection. Cocker's lyrics are mostly focused on the everyday things of life (especially frustrated love, but with an original take on the subject) and are accompanied by traditional indie guitar, but also by some less traditional keyboard sounds, giving a slightly more 'electric' sound than the other Britpop bands. Cocker's vocals are very distinctive, and he often subsides into a semi-talking voice.

4 *Disco 2000*, Pulp

CD2: 10

Listen to *Disco 2000* by Pulp, taken from the album *Different Class* (1995).

a) How do Cocker's lyrics paint the picture of being an awkward teenager?

b) How does the instrumental backing support Cocker's delivery of the lyrics?

c) What similarities can you find between *Disco 2000* and *Parklife*?

Oasis

Noel Gallagher began his music career in 1989 as a roadie for The Inspiral Carpets. He gained the position by failing an audition as the new singer for the band at the end of 1988. The band took a liking to him and decided to take him on in a slightly less elevated role. After seeing his younger brother Liam's band (an early incarnation of Oasis) at a gig, he decided to take over the management of the band in addition to his duties for The Inspiral Carpets. He took control of the songwriting and gave the band a much more professional approach to their rehearsals (they could barely play their instruments at this stage). Eventually, The Inspiral Carpets' success dwindled and they had to dispense with Noel's services as a roadie, so Oasis became his sole focus. By this stage, he was also the band's lead guitarist. They signed to Creation Records, run by the colourful character Alan McGee, in 1993. After the release of their debut album *Definitely Maybe* in 1994, Oasis went from strength to strength, becoming exceedingly popular with the record-buying public.

Noel Gallagher performing for Oasis with his Union Jack guitar.

5 *Supersonic*, Oasis
CD2: 11

Listen to the track *Supersonic* by Oasis.

a) How is the scraping sound in the intro achieved?

b) Describe the phrase structure of the verse.

c) Write out the structure of the song.

d) What elements give this song its powerful driving feel?

e) What elements of the song make it sound 'British'?

The Beatles' influence

Oasis are the Britpop band who most openly acknowledge The Beatles as a major influence. Their song *Don't Look Back in Anger* (from the album *(What's the Story) Morning Glory?* (1995)) has an opening piano riff that is reminiscent of John Lennon's *Imagine* (1975). On their third album, a collection of B-sides and previously unreleased material entitled *The Masterplan* (1998), they include a cover of a Beatles song *I am the Walrus*. They are happy to admit borrowing from The Beatles, and this serves to reinforce their credentials as a very British band.

Other bands such as The Jam, The Who and The Rolling Stones have all been listed as influences by members of Oasis, Blur, Suede and Pulp. This 1960s guitar-based British rock band influence is an important part of the Britpop sound.

6 Songwriting

To write in a style reminiscent of any of the four major Britpop bands requires a certain amount of ability on the guitar, and the following task is written from the perspective of a guitarist. It is worth noting that, certainly in the case of Oasis, the members of the band were not overly competent on their instruments at the start of their career and restricted their songs to fairly simple bare chord progressions. Some songs were based on repetitive riffs, while others were melodies over a chord sequence.

a) Using only the shapes of E major and A major, and barring at any point on the fretboard, compose a four-bar chord sequence. The song should be in 4/4 time with two chord changes per bar.

b) Choose a topic for your lyrics. It should be something everyday, or it should be an alternative view of a frustrated love situation.

c) Brainstorm your chosen topic by writing any words or phrases that come to mind on a piece of paper.

d) Arrange your brainstorm ideas into groups of linked ideas.

e) Take a group of ideas that has the most catchy lyric for the chorus. Edit the lyrics carefully so that they make rhythmic sense when you speak them over your chord sequence.

f) Fit a melody to your lyrics that works over the chord sequence. Often this will be pentatonic, taking the five notes of the major pentatonic scale of E major (or whatever your tonic key is). It may be slightly more complicated, using notes from the chords under the melody (for example, when the chord is G major, you might use G, B or D, but if the chord then changes to A major, the melody note would be A, C# or E) or you may combine both techniques. Songs in this style often ignore the odd clash between harmony and melody or even make a feature of such a clash.

g) Write a second chord sequence to use as your verse. This should normally be fairly simple as the lyrics change for each verse.

h) Organize your remaining lyrics into verses and edit in the same way as you did for step e.

i) Finally, you need a simple sequence to use as a bridge (or middle 8). Often this consists of simply alternating between two chords. If you have been using just major shapes, you might now also introduce a minor seventh chord for variety. You might want to save some lyrics for this section, or just use it as an instrumental break.

j) Organize your ideas using one of the structural templates you wrote down from the listening tasks earlier on in the chapter. An introduction might help the listener to get into the song – this might just be an instrumental rendition of either the verse or chorus sequence or it might be an additional sequence that you bring back later on in your song.

k) Add additional instruments to accompany your song. The bass guitar will probably play basic root notes, following the barre chord pattern played on the guitar. The drums should play a similar pattern to those heard on the extracts; Britpop drumming is fairly straightforward but maintains a driving rhythm. Keyboards may be added if you wish, either following the same chords or adding an occasional riff for interest.

Britpop as a genre

Britpop does not have any definite musical elements that are common to all the music produced by the four main bands who define the style. Britpop is more about an Anglo-centric attitude. The big four bands all shared a sense of American bands taking over areas in the music industry where British bands used to reign supreme in the days of The Beatles, The Rolling Stones, The Jam and so on.

By the late 1980s, very few British bands were making any impact at all on the American market and, worse still, not a great deal of impact on the British market! With the advent of grunge from Seattle (and Nirvana in particular), American heavy rock reigned supreme. Britpop was partly a reaction to the domination of the British music scene by Seattle grunge and other American rock music. It is also a celebration of being British, consciously or unconsciously focusing on all things British, be it lyrically or in the music itself.

Another common trait shared by all the major bands in the genre is the lyrical focus. As Jarvis Cocker said, it is about finding the poetry in simple, everyday things (such as *Disco 2000*: 'Your house was very small, with woodchip on the wall').

In terms of shared musical elements, the most common trait would be the avoidance of the blues cliché so common of the American rock bands; very few of the chord sequences are anything like the twelve-bar blues sequence. Many Britpop chord sequences are deceptively simple but with an added twist by adding an unexpected chord, or breakdown and so on. Guitar solos take a much less important role than is true of American rock, with the emphasis on a driving rhythm and the importance of the lyrics. All the major bands of the genre draw their main influences from the great British bands of the 1960s and the indie bands of the 1980s. The influence of The Smiths on all the Britpop bands cannot be overstated.

Area of Study 4:

Indian raga, African music and fusions

There are as many different types of world music as there are countries in the world, and most of these musical cultures have existed for thousands of years. Only over the last century have we really started to get to know and investigate music from all corners of the globe. With the advent of travel and mass communication, the world has become a much smaller place and we have been able to explore all aspects of different cultures, including food, dress, customs, beliefs and traditions as well as indigenous music.

World music is a vast subject. The people who specialize in the study of world music are called ethnomusicologists and they often spend years researching the music. They will live in the country among the people, recording and writing down the music they see and hear performed. They will also investigate the construction of the instruments as well as how they are played.

In this Area of Study you will be required to study three world music topics:
- Indian raga
- African music
- fusions.

Indian raga

Indian Classical music can be traced back at least two thousand years and is still flourishing today. This topic looks at the tradition of the rag and shows how this ancient system of Indian melody forms the basis for performances. This music has been passed down from generation to generation

An Indian music ensemble.

and is not written down or notated but learnt by memory. This method of learning is known as the oral tradition. African music is learnt in much the same way.

The study of Indian raga will highlight the three important ingredients of:
- melody – rag
- rhythm – tala
- drone accompaniment.

The skill in this music relies on the ability to improvise – that is, to make up music on the spot. The different sections of the raga, called the alap, jhor, jhalla and gat (or bandish) provide contrasts throughout the performance.

African music

The chapter on African music has three main strands:
- drumming music
- tribal chant or song
- instrumental music.

This chapter shows how common ideas and techniques are used in all types of African music. As with Indian music, African music is performed from memory and requires great skill in improvisation.

The drum is considered to be the most important and precious of all instruments and has many functions. The main role of the drum traditionally was for communication between tribal communities. Drumming was a central part of social gatherings, whether it was a wedding, funeral, gathering of chiefs and so on. Certain rhythm patterns had specific associations and therefore a particular type of rhythm had its own meaning. The famous 'talking drums' (called donno) could literally speak by producing different pitches through the stretching of the drum skin and thus imitating the vocal inflexions of the African tone languages.

African singing is also very much linked to community life and there are songs for all occasions, both happy and sad. These pieces are relatively simple, yet highly effective, and often use the common technique of 'call and response' as a means of providing a simple structure of a solo line answered by the whole tribe.

The instrumental music covers a vast area, but for your GCSE you will only have to look at the xylophone music, mbira pieces (thumb piano) and the music of the 21-string lute, known as the kora. In all three cases, the musical techniques used in these pieces are common to all types of African music.

Fusions

Any music that draws together at least two musical cultures is a fusion and this is a vast topic. One well-established fusion that is included in this book is bhangra, which incorporates Indian Classical music fused with Western dance music. The chapter also looks at the famous Paul Simon album *Graceland*, which features African music fused with American rock, and also *African Sanctus* by David Fanshawe, which fuses tape recordings of African music with a western choir and instrumentalists.

There are many other examples of fusion using Indian or African music styles. For example, Hans Zimmer's music from the film *The Power of One* is worth investigating too. Indian music is also a feature in the glamorous movie world in India known as Bollywood. These songs feature traditional Indian instruments and use notes from rags but fuse them into a popular music idiom suitable for the film industry.

Indian raga

In this topic you will learn about:

- the importance of improvising music as part of the oral tradition
- the rag as a form of Indian melody
- the tala as the basic cyclic rhythm pattern
- the musical characteristics of the different sections of a raga performance
- common Indian instruments and playing techniques.

Indian music has a long history going back more than two thousand years. It is closely linked to Hinduism and religious ideas and beliefs. The many Hindu gods are often worshipped through performances of **raga**, both vocal and instrumental. In particular, the god Shiva is associated with music and dance in Hinduism and there are many pieces in praise and honour of this particular deity.

The music of India can be divided into two great musical traditions:

- the music of northern India (the Hindustani tradition)
- the music of the south (the Carnatic tradition).

This chapter focuses on the Indian Classical tradition of the north.

The oral tradition

Unlike Western Classical music, Indian music is not written down as conventional musical notation. Instead it is taught through listening and playing by ear – called the oral tradition.

Indian families have a system of master–pupil teaching known as a **gharana**. A father might teach his son how to play through an intensive course involving listening and memorizing. The son would then pass on his skills to the next generation and so on.

Glossary

gharana in Indian music, the extended musical family in which pupils learn from a master

raga improvised music in several contrasting sections, based on a series of notes from a particular rag. The final section (Gat/Bandish) is not improvised, but features the 'fixed composition'

Elements of a raga

The three most common elements in Indian Classical music are:

- the melody – made up (improvised) from notes of a particular rag; they are sung by a voice or played by an instrument such as the sitar or sarod
- the drone – a supporting 'drone' of usually one or two notes provided by the tambura
- the rhythm – a repetitive, cyclic rhythm pattern played by the tabla drums.

Indian classical music is concerned with melody and the development of a musical line. It is **linear** in concept. The harmony is basic and static, comprising only the drone notes which are primarily for intonational purposes.

Indian instruments

The voice

There are many different Indian instruments but the most highly regarded is the human voice, as in Indian philosophy it is thought that by singing it is possible to talk directly to the gods. All other instruments are ranked according to how close their sound or timbre resembles the sound of the voice.

The sitar

This is the most well-known plucked string instrument. It has seven principal metal strings of which two are used as drone notes, below which there are up to a dozen loose fretted strings called 'sympathetic' because they vibrate in sympathy when the top strings are plucked. This gives the traditional 'twangy' sound that makes the instrument instantly recognizable. The main strings are played by plucking with a wire plectrum. Two common playing techniques are sliding between notes (called **meend**, or mind) and rapid scale-like flourishes called **tan**.

The sarangi

This is smaller than the sitar and differs in that it is fretless and uses a bow rather than plucking. A bit like a violin, the instrument has a gentle tone and is often used to accompany singers.

Glossary

linear music that is conceived in terms of lines of melody, rather than in chords or harmony

meend (or mind) in Indian music, the sliding effects between notes

tan the rapid scalic flourishes on the sitar, sarod or sarangi

A sitar.

The sarangi.

The sarod

The sarod is also smaller than the sitar but like a sitar it has two sets of strings to create the distorted effect common to the sitar. It is fretless and has a metal fingerboard so that the player can slide up and down the strings to obtain different notes. The instrument has a lower range and heavier tone than the sitar.

The tambura

A simple instrument with only four strings and resonator, it is used to provide the drone notes to accompany the singer or instrumentalist.

The tabla

This is a small set of two drums of different sizes, one for each hand. Both drumheads are made of skin, and the black centre circle that you can see is made of a paste of iron filings and flour. The drums play the chosen rhythm cycle known as the **tala**.

The tabla drums.

Other instruments

Many other instruments are used, the most common being two woodwind types of flute and oboe. The flute (**bansuri**) and oboe (**shenhai**) do not have keys like modern Western equivalents but a series of holes. The players skilfully produce a wide range of pitches by half covering the holes and varying the blowing. Sliding effects, as on string instruments, are also possible too.

> **Glossary**
>
> **bansuri** an Indian flute without keys
>
> **shenai** a double reed Indian instrument, similar to the oboe
>
> **tala** the chosen rhythmic cycle of beats in Indian music played on the tabla drums

Melody – the rag

The rag is the melody on which the music is improvised. This is a cross between a collection of pitches and a scale. Like a scale, a rag ascends and descends, but the actual pitches often differ in each direction. Unlike the pattern of scales in Western Classical music with the same number of notes, the ascending and descending notes in a rag can vary. Some rags have just five notes rather like the pentatonic scale.

Drone notes

Here are two other rags: one an early morning rag called
Vibhas and the other a night-time rag called *Kalyan*.

There are more than 200 different rags in existence in Indian
Classical music, and each has a particular mood (called a
rasa) associated with it. Not only are there morning and night
rags, but also celebration rags, seasonal rags and even some
associated with certain feelings and emotions. Others are even
deemed to be male or female! There is virtually a rag for every
occasion. The chosen rag will be used as the melodic material
in a full raga performance and the music is then made up by
the performers. This technique of making up music without
notation is called improvisation.

Glossary

rasa the particular mood
created by the sounds of
the pitches in a particular
rag

1 Rag time!

a) Use any of the three rag examples given on pages 108–109 as a basis for a short musical
    improvisation on your own instrument. You do not need to write anything down, but try to
    develop a melody from the given notes of your rag.
b) Work with a partner. One of you can use the suggested drone notes on these pages and
    play them on a keyboard instrument or a cello to accompany the melody improvisation.

Rhythm – the tala

Rhythm provided by the small tabla drums is organized into repeating rhythmic cycles called tala. The most common tala is the **teental** (or tintal), which is a sixteen beat pattern (called **matras**) organized in four bars as 4 + 4 + 4 + 4. There are many other talas with different numbers of beats per cycle, including 6, 7, 8, 10, 12, 14 and 16.

The complex rhythms sound exciting when played against this steady beat by both the tabla player as well as the instrumentalist (or singer). These rhythm patterns, called **bols**, are independent of the beat and can be inventive, displacing accents off the beat to create **syncopations**.

However, these rhythms must start and end together precisely on the first beat of the cycle, called **sam**. In a raga performance, this can lead to exciting competitions between instrumentalist and drummer as they attempt to copy and outdo each others' clever and novel rhythmic ideas while still keeping within the cycle of beats – a sort of musical duel!

Glossary

bols independent rhythm parts that go against the main beat of the cycle

matras the individual beats in a rhythmic cycle

sam in Indian music, the first beat of the rhythmic cycle

syncopations notes accented off the beat

teental the common 16 beat (4+4+4+4) rhythmic cycle in Indian raga

2 Tala time for three

a) Work in a group of three. Choose three different percussion instruments and try your hand at improvising exciting rhythms against a constant beat provided by the matras (player 1).

b) Use the common teental pattern of beats: 4 + 4 + 4 + 4.
   - One player keeps the beat (matras).
   - Players two and three play independent rhythm parts (bols).
   - All three parts must synchronize on beat 1 (sam).
   - Make sure that you change parts otherwise player one will lose interest fast!

Beat	1	2	3	4	5	6	7	8	9	10	11	12	13	14	15	16	1 (Repeat)
Player 1 Matras	Sam	P	L	A	Y		ON			ALL		BEATS					Sam
Player 2 Bols	Sam	F	R	E	E			P	A	R	T						Sam
Player 3 Bols	Sam	F	R	E	E			P	A	R	T						Sam

The structure of a raga performance

A raga performance usually has a structure based on defined sections called the **alap**, **jhor**, **jhalla** and **gat** (called a **bandish** if the piece is vocal).

However:

- some sections can be omitted, for example a raga might just have an alap and a gat
- raga performances can vary vastly in time – up to five hours in some cases! Some performances can last all night!

The table below shows the main characteristics of each section.

Section	Tempo	Metre/rhythm	Musical features
Alap	Slow	No sense of metre (free time)	Soloist 'explores' the notes of the rag, setting the mood, accompanied by the tambura drone. The music is improvised
Jhor	Steady medium	A real sense of a regular pulse is established	Improvised music becomes more rhythmic. Music becomes more elaborate and the tempo increases
Jhalla	Fast	Fast pulse with exciting rhythms	High point in piece. Virtuoso display using advanced playing techniques
Gat/ bandish	Moderate to fast	Tabla drums introduce the rhythmic cycle 'tala'	The 'fixed composition' is introduced. In the case of a vocal piece, a song, in an instrumental piece, a prepared solo. Musical dialogue takes place between the instrumentalist and drummer, as well as improvised flourishes on the prepared melodic line

Glossary

alap the opening unmetred and improvised section of an Indian raga

bandish the last section of a vocal raga performance

gat the final section of an instrumental raga performance. This features a 'fixed composition' which is performed with some improvisations

jhala the third section of a raga performance, including the climax. Features include a lively tempo and virtuoso display of improvisatory skills

jhor the second section in a typical raga performance. In medium tempo featuring improvisation by the soloist

3 Raga Jogeshwari

CD2: 12–14

'Jogeshwari' is the Goddess of Yoga. The full performance of this raga lasts over 50 minutes and has an alap, a jhor and two contrasting gat sections. Listen to the extracts from the alap, jhor and the second gat sections of the raga.

The following questions relate to the alap section.

a) Name the two instruments that you can hear in this section.

b) What is the purpose of the ever-present drone in this music?

c) How would you describe the tempo and metre of the music?

d) This section of an Indian raga is improvised. What does the performer attempt to do in this opening section?

The following questions relate to the jhor section.

e) State *two* ways in which the music of this section differs from the opening gat section.

f) What happens to the tempo towards the end of the extract?

The following questions relate to the second gat section.

g) What new instrument plays in this section and what does it play?

h) Mention *one* way in which this section differs from the alap and jhor sections.

4 Soja Re (Go to sleep) and *Guru Bandana*

CD2: 15 & 16

The first extract features the sarangi played by Sultan Khan, who also sings the vocal part. The other performer is Zakir Hussain, who plays the tabla. *Soja Re* is a traditional Rajasthani lullaby.

Listen to the first extract.

a) What is the mood of this piece and how is it conveyed in the music?

b) Describe the part played by the tabla.

c) What are the two different musical roles of the sarangi in this piece?

Now listen to the second extract featuring Ali Akbar Khan on the tambura and Asha Bhosle singing.

d) Mention two differences between these two vocal pieces.

e) Which piece did you prefer? Give three musical reasons for your choice.

5 Gat or bandish?

Compose either a gat (a short instrumental composition) or a bandish (a short song). You can use the notes from one of the ragas in this chapter or you can compose your own.
In the case of the vocal piece, you can write some words or you can just use vowel sounds (this is called vocalize). You will also need to include in your composition:

• a rhythm part (tala) to be played on a drum

• a drone part to be played on any keyboard instrument (or a cello). Finally, perform your pieces to one another in class.

African music

In this topic you will learn about:

- the rich and diverse musical cultures of Sub-Saharan Africa and the social importance of African music
- rhythm patterns and procedures in African drumming music and the role of the master drummer
- 'call and response' techniques found in African choral song
- African instruments and their construction
- the common features of African instrumental music.

African music in society

Music plays an important role in many African societies and is used to communicate a multitude of different feelings and emotions. In many African religions, musical sound is thought to be one of the most direct ways in which the gods (deities) and humans can impose order on the world. Music is always part of any social gathering, be it to celebrate the harvest, a birthday, wedding, funeral or a gathering of chiefs. On all these occasions it is often combined with speech, dance and vibrant costumes to produce exciting and dramatic performances in which everyone is expected to take part.

Common elements of African music

Sub-Saharan Africa covers a region of 50 nations, each with its own traditions. So, the music of this area is extremely rich, colourful and diverse. However, it is possible to identify some common elements such as:

- repetition
- **improvisation**
- **polyphony**
- **call and response**.

It is also possible to place the music in three broad strands: drumming, choral song (tribal music) and instrumental music (which includes the xylophone, mbira and kora music).

Glossary

call and response simple form comprising a solo (call) followed by a group answering phrase (response)

improvise make up music spontaneously

polyphony texture featuring two or more parts, each having a melody line and sounding together - creates a multilayered texture

African drumming

The drum has always been considered the most important instrument in Africa. It has been a means of communication, with certain rhythm patterns meaning different things. Thus, a slow beat could signal a sad occasion such as a funeral. The drum also has religious significance and is used in all forms of ceremonies, including weddings, funerals and the celebrations of the annual harvest.

The Royal Burundi Drummers.

There are hundreds of different drums and their names vary from region to region and even from one tribe to the next. The most common drum is called the **djembe**. This is a single-headed instrument shaped like a goblet and is made in a range of sizes to produce different pitches. The drums can be played on their own, but will frequently be heard in ensembles where there is usually a solo drum played by the master drummer and a set of accompanying drums. The most famous of these groups is called The Royal Burundi Drummers.

As well as the single-headed drums, there are double-headed drums that can be played using sticks. The drums' heads have different sizes and will produce two different pitches – for example, the **dundun**. One of the other famous types of drum in West Africa – the **donno** – is known as the talking drum. This is held under the arm and played with the hands.

The dundun drum.

Different sounds can be made using different playing techniques such as:

- playing hands on the skin of the drum; different sounds are made when the fingers are open or closed
- playing hands on the wooden edge of the drum
- using sticks to create a sharp staccato sound
- stretching the drum membrane to produce a range of pitches, particularly on the donno.

Glossary

djembe goblet-shaped drum from West Africa

donno hourglass shaped 'talking drum' held under the arm and played with the hand

dundun double-headed drum (in several different sizes) played with sticks

tempo the speed of the music

A typical performance

This music is founded on the oral tradition and therefore has no musical notation. The master drummer stands in the centre of the ensemble and is responsible for directing the whole performance. He will be surrounded by other drummers and percussion instruments. The master drummer will signal to the other players when he is ready to start, often with a vocal cry followed by a short rhythmic solo to set the mood and **tempo** of the music.

This is called a cue and the other players will then come in together to play the response. The response could be an exact copy or even a different rhythm entirely. This 'call and response' technique is a main feature of tribal music. Cueing will happen throughout the music and creates a structure of contrasted sections. The music is essentially a series of variations on rhythmic patterns.

During the course of the piece, the master drummer will signal to the other individual players to perform a solo. This again will be a variation or development of the original rhythm pattern and will lead to further rhythmic developments by the players. A steady continuous beat, called the timeline, is often played by the master drummer, and there may also be a percussion rattle or bells, the most common being the agogo bells.

The complex rhythms played by the drummers create polyrhythms, often with stresses that conflict with each other and with the steady constant beat of the timeline – creating **cross rhythms**. The result is a **polyrhythmic texture**.

The music will usually increase in tension as the piece progresses, and the tempo and dynamics will vary from section to section to provide interest and variety in the music. It is the responsibility of the master drummer to control the changes and make sure that the music never becomes monotonous or dull.

Some of these performances can take up to five hours or even longer, and as well as solo drumming spots, which give the individual players a chance to show off their skills of improvisation, there is often movement and dance.

Glossary

cross rhythms rhythms that literally cross the usual pattern of accented and unaccented beats creating irregular accents and syncopated effects. Groupings of notes can go over bar lines too

polyrhythmic texture texture made up of many different rhythms

1 *Akan Drumming*, Pan African Orchestra   CD2: 17

Now listen to the piece of African drumming.

a) Identify as many common features of African drumming already mentioned as possible.

b) What mood or feelings do you get from listening to this piece?

c) What do you notice about the tempo and dynamics during the course of the music?

d) How is the hypnotic effect of the music achieved?

2 Create some African drumming

Work in groups of four to six players to create a piece of African drumming. Each player will need a drum, tambourine or bongos. Nominate one player as the master drummer.

a) Sit in a circle with the master drummer in the centre.

b) The master drummer gives an opening cue, shouting out 'Kundum', and then plays an opening rhythm.

c) The master drummer cues in the rest of the group to repeat this pattern together.

d) The master drummer then calls out the name of a drummer at random to perform a short solo, which is then repeated by the rest of the group.

e) The piece ends when the last player has played solo and the group has responded.

3 Performing rhythms

Work in three groups to create a repetitive rhythm of two bars.

Group A creates a rhythm of three beats per bar, stressed **1** 2 3.

Group B creates a rhythm of four beats per bar, stressed **1** 2 3 **4**.

Group C has a rhythm of five beats per bar, stressed **1** 2 3 **4** 5.

The teacher will act as master drummer and will provide the timeline with bells. The master drummer will start the ensemble off by establishing a steady beat and then cueing in each group in turn.

Next, try to invent more complex patterns using dotted (reverse dotted) and syncopated rhythms.

African choral singing

Sub-Saharan musical traditions are centred around singing. Many Africans believe that the music serves as a link to the spirit world. Singing is a vital part of everyday life and is heard at religious ceremonies, rituals and celebrations. Singing unites whole tribal communities and everyone takes part, whether they have a good singing voice or not!

The songs provide a means of communication. African languages are **tone languages** – that is, the **pitch** level (high or low) determines the meaning of the words. Therefore the melodies and rhythms can be made to fit in pitch outlines to match the meanings and speech rhythms of the words of the song.

Glossary

pitch how high or low a note(s) sounds

tone languages in African music, languages made up of only a few pitches, called tone languages. The pitch level determines the meaning of the words

Below are some common features of African songs.

- The basic form of the songs is call and response.
- The melodies are usually short and simple, and repeated over and over.
- Melodies are usually in a scale of only four, five, six or seven different **tones**.
- These melodies can be changed at will by other singers so that what we end up with is a theme and variations.
- Performers can improvise new melodies while the other singers continue the original melody. It is common to have different melodies sounding simultaneously resulting in polyphony and polyphonic textures.
- Often the music can be sung in rounds. For example, in Zulu choral music, individual voices enter at different points in a continuous cycle, overlapping in a complex and ever-changing musical **texture**.
- Harmony, which will vary from tribe to tribe. In some communities, the voices sing only in unison or parallel **octaves**, with the odd fourth or fifth. However, other groups will freely harmonize in thirds or fourths and can even sing in two or three different parts.

Glossary

octave the interval of eight notes, e.g. C to C eight notes higher

texture the number of parts in a piece of music and how they relate to one another. There are several distinct types such as **homophony**, **polyphony**, **monophony** and **heterophony** (see glossary on page 155)

tone the interval of two semitones, e.g. F to G is made up of F to F# (a semitone) and F# to G (a semitone)

4 *Mbube*, Solomon Linda's Original Evening Birds, and *Kangivumanga*, Ladysmith Black Mambazo *CD2: 18 & 19*

Listen to the two African songs.

The first track is called *Mbube* and is performed by Solomon Linda's Original Evening Birds. This is an old recording from 1939 and was the first commercial recording to sell over 100,000 copies.

More up to date, but in the same genre, is the second song, *Kangivumanga* (1988), performed by Ladysmith Black Mambazo. This group has come to represent the traditional music of the Zulus of South Africa. This music is called **isicathamiya**. 'Black Mambazo' means 'black axe' and refers to the axe that will defeat all opponents in singing competitions. This ambitious group achieved worldwide success and has released more than 30 records, all of which have gone gold.

Glossary

isicathamiya the traditional vocal music of the Zulus of South Africa

a) Which musical features of African singing (outlined above) could you detect in both of these pieces?

b) What differences did you notice in the two performances?

c) Which piece did you prefer? Give at least two musical reasons for your choice.

5 Call and response song

Working on your own or with a partner, compose a call and response song like the pieces you listened to in Task 4. Choose your own subject. It could be a protest song about having too much homework to do, or even a protest about having to do this task. When you have finished, arrange a performance with your class.

6 Call and response

Perform this simple African song in class.

African instrumental music

There are many different instruments in African music and they vary from region to region. The different types of drums are called **membranophones** (because they have a skin). The other main types of instruments can be broadly categorized as follows.

Idiophones (resonant/solid)	Aerophones (wind)	Chordophones (strings)
Rattles (shakera)	Flutes (bamboo, horn)	Zithers
Bells	Ocarinas	Lutes (kora)
Mbira (thumb piano)	Panpipes	Harps
Xylophones (balophone)	Horns (from animal tusks)	Lyres
Clap sticks	Trumpets (wood, metal)	Musical bows
Slit gongs	Pipes (single and double reeds)	
Stamping tubes	Whistle	

There is also body percussion, which includes hand clapping and foot stamping, as well as vocal effects, such as shouting and other **vocables**.

The instruments are selected for performance according to the nature and mood of the instrumental music or song. These instruments have more complex tuning systems than used in vocal music and are capable of playing quite demanding rhythms and melodies. As in the drumming music, the melody often consists of several different parts that interlock and overlap to form polyrhythmic structures.

Three of the most common instruments are the xylophone (or balophone), the mbira (a thumb piano) and the kora (a 21-string lute).

Glossary

membranophones category of instruments that have a drum skin (membrane)

vocables effects made by the voice, using vowel sounds such as 'eh', 'ah', 'oh' etc

Xylophones

You will be familiar with xylophones, as they are often used in schools. These African instruments are made in several different sizes, providing a wide range of pitches from the deep resonant bass notes up to the high pitches of the small xylophones. The wooden bars are set on a framework and to allow the bars to vibrate and resound, a membrane is needed between the bars and the frame. On your school instruments, this is most likely to be rubber, but the African instruments use naturally occurring materials such as orange peel!

Mbira

This is an ancient instrument, thought to have been around for at least a thousand years. Its full name is 'mbira dzavadzimu', which means 'mbira of the ancient spirits'. It is an important instrument and is used at religious rituals as well as social gatherings.

Mbira – the thumb piano.

The mbira has 22 metal strips of varying length (although this can vary in number from 20–28). These are fixed to a hardwood soundboard and this is placed in a resonating chamber made of a calabash, called the deze, which amplifies the sound. The keys are arranged in three tiers (or ranks). The instrument is often called the thumb piano because the two thumbs stroke the keys downwards and the right forefinger then plucks them back up.

To create a buzzing and distorted sound, the deze is strung with metal beads or shells (or even bottle tops), which vibrate in sympathy when the metal keys are played. Tuning varies considerably from one instrument to the next and only if two instruments are played together does the tuning need to match.

The kora

This instrument originates from West Africa (Mali, Gambia, Guinea, Sierra Leone and Senegal). The kora is a complex instrument, looking rather like a harp–lute or guitar. It has between 10 and 23 strings, although most kora have 21 strings (or 22, where the extra is a bass string). It plays a range of about three-and-a-half octaves. It is one of the most melodic of all African instruments and sounds with a harp-like quality. It is often used as an accompanying instrument to songs by the **Griot** families.

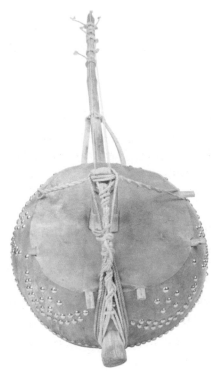

Kora – 21 string lute.

Traditionally, the strings were made of gut or strips of leather, but now they are made from nylon fishing lines. These produce a sharper sound and are arranged into two parallel groups. The strings are plucked by the thumb and forefinger of each hand while the remaining fingers hold the vertical hand posts. The body of the instrument is a calabash gourd cut in half and covered with a taut cowhide membrane, which helps to amplify the bass sounds. The long neck has leather bands attached at the top for tuning the strings just like a guitar. The different regions of West Africa have their own tuning systems and each region has its own playing styles and regional repertoire.

Glossary

Griot African Music. In Mandika society, this was a school of musicians who preserved the stories from its history through songs accompanied by the Kora

Common features of African instrumental music

The five common features of African instrumental music are repetition (including **ostinato**), improvisation, cyclic structures, polyphonic textures and intertwining melodies.

In the xylophone music of the Chopi people of Mozambique, the repetition of melodic and rhythmic patterns, called ostinati, are a common feature as well as improvised melodies.

7 *Induna Indaba*, Chopi people of Mozambique   CD2: 20

Listen to the 1996 piece called *Induna Indaba* (Gathering of Chiefs).

a) What other instruments, apart from the xylophones, can you hear?

b) What is the main musical feature in the music played by the xylophones?

c) Describe the tempo and mood of this music.

d) How many different sizes of xylophone are in the ensemble?

The mbira music of the Zezuru group or the Shona people of Zimbabwe also uses repeated ostinato patterns upon which the musician then improvises on the core pattern. The music is cyclic and contains many mbira, often with contrasting and syncopated rhythms. The music progresses through a process of very gradual change over a period of time, just like minimalist music (see pages 47–57). In a group, the instruments produce polyphonic textures where two parts include the **kushaura** (leading part) and the **kutsinhira** (the intertwining part). Although cyclic, the performers do not consider any one point in the cycle as the beginning or the end, so they start and finish wherever they want to. Hosho, a pair of rattles, play a constant rhythm like the timeline of the agogo bells in the drumming music.

8 *Chemutengure*, Dumisani Maraire and Ephat Mujuru   CD2: 21

Now listen to the mbira piece, *Chemutengure* (2000).

a) How would you describe the dynamics in this piece?

b) What is unusual about the sound produced by these instruments?

c) Describe the texture of the music.

d) What mood does this music conjure up?

The kora sounds like a melodic harp and is used to accompany songs. Simple repetitive rhythms and solo improvisations based on the melody line called **brimintingo** are a feature. There is an ostinato line, also, below the melody called the **kumbengo**.

9 *Yamfa*, Toumani Diabaté amd Ballake Sissoko

CD2: 22

Listen to this piece for two koras called *Yamfa*.

a) Describe the melody part as fully as you can.

b) What musical device can be heard in the bass part?

c) How would you describe the tempo of the music?

d) What family of instruments does the kora belong to?

e) Name *one* feature of this piece that is common to the other two extracts you have just listened to.

10 Ostinato/ostinati

This task can be done either using a music notation package such as Sibelius, or on manuscript paper with a pencil, rubber and ruler.

a) Set out the three staves joined together and rule eight bars. Choose your own time signature.

b) Part 1 = xylophone melody;
Part 2 = xylophone ostinato 1;
Part 3 = xylophone ostinato 2.

c) Compose the two ostinato parts using the notes C, D, E, G and A. Make both ostinatos either one or two bars long and try to make them different.

d) Write a catchy melody again only using the pentatonic notes of C, D, E, G and A.

e) If you do this using Sibelius, you can cut and paste your ostinati and hear your completed piece using playback.

f) If you do it on manuscript paper, try to perform your piece on three different size xylophones, glockenspiels or three keyboards.

11 On the spot ostinati!

Working in groups of six to eight, use a selection of school xylophones and percussion instruments and improvise an ostinato piece just like *Induna Indaba* (see Task 7).

a) Use only the notes C, D, E, G and A to create a pentatonic scale. You can take out the F and B bars on the xylophones to make life easier.

b) One person needs to direct, bringing in each part one at a time to build up a musical texture. Just as in the listening piece, one or two of you might like to improvise on your own instruments.

Fusions

Musical fusion was a twentieth-century musical phenomenon and, as the name implies, is where two or more music styles have been merged together to create a new fused sound featuring elements from both musical traditions. Although there are many fusions around today, this topic includes only those that use Indian or African music in combination with another musical style. One of the most well known of these is bhangra – a fusion of Indian Classical music and Western dance music.

This chapter also looks at two songs from the album *Graceland* by Paul Simon in which African music is fused with American rock, as well as David Fanshawe's choral work *African Sanctus*.

Bhangra

Bhangra originates from the Punjabi region of India and was the original folk music of the peasant farm workers. The music was named after **bhang**, which was the hemp the farmers grew and then harvested. To relieve the monotony of their work, the farmers would sing local folk melodies to the accompaniment of a double-headed drum, called the **dhol**. This kept the repetitive rhythm or beat of the music going in a triplet crotchet-quaver rhythm, called the **chaal**. This is notated as shown below.

This rhythm is virtually unchanged today and provides the essential bass groove on drum machines that is a feature of the music.

Glossary

bhang hemp crop harvested by Punjabi peasant farmer workers that led to the name of their folk music called Bhangra

chaal the basic eight beat rhythmic cycle used in Bhangra

dhol large double-headed barrel drum, used in the Punjabi region of India in performances of Bhangra

The melodies were fairly straightforward, easy to remember and were passed down in the oral tradition from one generation to the next. This music has parallels with the early blues work songs sung by the African slaves in the United States of America in that music was used to relieve the tedium of working in the fields. In the Punjab, the songs grew in popularity, and, as with the early blues songs, their popularity spread to the towns where the music was used for entertainment.

Bhangra as we know it today is really a British–Asian creation. Since the early 1980s, Asian immigrants living in the UK wanted to forge their own musical identity in the community, and the traditional Indian bhangra fused with British pop dance music provided the answer. It is an exciting fusion that has grown over recent years into a significant genre in its own right.

Musical features of bhangra

Bhangra uses elements from modern club dance technology such as looped and sampled material, drum machines and so on, alongside the traditional elements of the original bhangra songs. Some of the common musical features are as follows.

Indian bhangra		British pop dance music
Chaal rhythm	unchanged on	drum machines
Punjabi language	often mixed with	English in the lyrics
Indian instruments	mixed with	Western pop instruments

The melody is often quite repetitive and is treated in the traditional verse/chorus structure, common to British pop songs.

Bhangra has changed from its original form as a type of Punjabi folk music that is essentially a song to one that is primarily a dance form.

1 *Chargiye*, Bombay Talkie

Listen to the bhangra dance track called *Chargiye*, taken from the album *Judgement Day* (2000) by Bombay Talkie.

a) Identify features of the fusion of the two musical cultures using the following three headings:
- melody and lyrics
- rhythm and **tempo**
- instruments.

b) Discuss your findings as a class with your teacher.

Glossary

tempo the speed of the music

2 A bhangra bop

Composing a piece of fusion is difficult unless you have both Indian and Western instruments. However, if you have a sequencing program on the computers in your music department, for example Cubase, you can use those for composing fusion.

a) Using a sequencing programme, build up your own bhangra piece based on the foundation of the characteristic chaal rhythm.

b) Build up different rhythmic and melodic tracks over the chaal rhythm.

c) When you write the melody, use only the following notes taken from the kalyan **raga**:
C#, E, F#, G#, A, B, C# and D.

d) The final number of tracks you decide to write is up to you.

e) Play back your finished sequenced composition to the rest of your class.

f) How effective was your fusion? Did it sound like authentic bhangra?

Glossary

raga improvised music in several contrasting sections, based on a series of notes from a particular rag

Rock and African music fusion

There are many fusions that use elements from Indian or African music combined with another musical style or styles. This section looks at two examples – that found on the *Graceland* album (1986), by Paul Simon, and *African Sanctus* by David Fanshawe.

In the 1980s, a friend of Paul Simon's sent him a tape of African music. He was inspired by the joyful spirit of the vocals which reminded him of 1950s American rock and roll. He began to immerse himself in the sounds of South African mbaqanqa music. Some of the tracks on his subsequent album, *Graceland*, were actually recorded in South Africa. Other tracks were recorded in studios in the UK and USA. He involved African musicians, including the band Ladysmith Black Mambazo (see Task 4 on page 117), who added a real sense of vitality and spirit to the music.

The title track of the album describes a visit to Graceland, the famous home of Elvis Presley in Memphis, Tennessee. Using this title for his album, Paul Simon makes a connection between the two musical styles – contemporary American rock and roll and South African music.

Following the release and commercial success of *Graceland* (the album of eleven tracks sold over fifteen million copies and won a Grammy for Album of the Year), Paul Simon took the musicians who played on the album on his 'Born at the Right Time' tour. He said about this music that 'the concept was new, taking players from all over, and fusing them together in the big band sound'.

3 *Under African Skies* and *Homeless*, Paul Simon

Find a copy of the album *Graceland* (1986) and listen to the two tracks *Under African Skies* and *Homeless*.

a) Use the headings 'American rock' and 'African music', and see how many musical elements you can spot in both songs.

David Fanshawe

In 1969, David Fanshawe hitch-hiked his way through the Sudan and into Uganda making tape recordings of African tribal music which were later used in his famous work *African Sanctus*. Fanshawe fused traditional African music with his choral mass setting to create a piece which, in his own words 'would express my adventures and love of people in a composition where African music, African songs and dances, religious recitations and ceremonies would live within the heart of a work conceived along 'Western' lines in the form of a Mass.'

The work was first performed in this version for soprano solo, choir, percussion and African tapes in July 1972 by the Saltarello Choir at St. John's Smith Square, London. Since then, Fanshawe has added other optional parts including lead and bass guitar, rock drum kit, ethnic drums and electric organ.

4 *African Sanctus*, David Fanshawe
CD2: 24

The Bwala Dance is the Royal Dance of Uganda and you will hear a recording of the Acholi people singing alongside a Western choir and instrumentalists on this track.

a) As you listen to the whole track, try to identify as many African and Western instruments, voices and sounds as possible. Write your answers under the two separate headings 'African' and 'Western.'

Preparing your coursework

In this topic you will learn about:
- the requirements of the specification
- how to choose a performance piece
- what examiners look for in a good performance/composition
- understanding the brief for a composition
- what makes a good composition.

How your course is assessed

GCSE Music for Edexcel is assessed by three papers:
Performing (Paper 1), **Composing** (Paper 2) and
Listening and Appraising (Paper 3).

Paper	% of GCSE	Assessment method
Performing	30%	Moderated coursework
Composing	30%	Moderated coursework
Listening and Appraising	40%	External examination

Performing and Composing are assessed through moderated
coursework, which is sent to the moderator in the first week of
May in the second year of your course (although your teacher
will require it long before this to mark it). Listening and
Appraising is assessed through a written exam in late May or
early June.

You are expected to have completed all the work for your GCSE
by yourself. Your teacher can assist you by teaching you how to
compose, guide you through the topics covered in the course,
give you some ideas on how to improve your performance
pieces, accompany you for your performance pieces and so on,
but your teacher cannot **do** any work for you that you intend
to submit for marking. Any assistance you receive beyond what
is normally expected needs to be explained in full on the forms
used to submit your work to the moderator.

Paper 1 – Performing

For this paper, Edexcel requires you to submit the following.

% of GCSE	Requirement	What can be submitted
15%	**One** solo performance	Traditional solo performance Solo improvisation Sequenced performance
15%	**One** ensemble performance	Traditional ensemble performance Improvising as part of an ensemble Multi-track recording Directing an ensemble

Both pieces need to be recorded onto a CD/MD or cassette. You need to submit a copy of the music you used to play the piece (either in notated form or a copy of the professional recording). You can re-record your pieces throughout the course until you are satisfied with the quality of your performances.

Traditional solo performance

A solo performance is what the title suggests – a performance featuring one soloist. Backing tracks or accompaniments can be used where appropriate. If a solo piece should contain an accompaniment, then this should be present on the recording submitted to the moderator.

If backing tracks are used, they *must not* contain the part to be assessed. For example, for vocalists, it is *not* acceptable to sing along with the original CD. It is perfectly acceptable to sing along to a professional backing track with the original vocal removed, or to use a MIDI file as the backing track (with the guide vocal track muted). It is possible to download MIDI files from the Internet (there are many free collections in addition to the commercial ones). Bass players, guitarists and drummers might also find this useful.

Solo improvisation

A solo improvisation can be in any style, but must always be well thought through. Your improvisation should:
- have a clear structure
- use and show development of the stimulus material
- have very little waffle or padding
- demonstrate what you are capable of without going beyond your abilities

- be a suitable length (not go on for ever or last for just two repeats of the stimulus)
- sound as if it has been rehearsed – there must be no hesitations.

Your choice of stimulus is important. A good choice will present lots of possibilities for further exploration. A bad choice might lock you into one idea or tempt you just to repeat it over and over with little alteration.

You need to practise the art of improvisation over the whole two years of the course if you want to attempt it as a solo performance option.

Asking your teacher to provide you with an improvising stimulus at the beginning of a lesson, working at it during the lesson and playing the piece to your teacher near the end of the lesson will help to invite comments about how well you did. This way you will build up your improvising skills and confidence.

Sequenced performance

This is the music technology option for the solo performance.

You have to submit a piece containing at least three different **timbres** (drums count as only one timbre, as does the piano). Your choice should be a complete piece or a suitable section – it should not stop part of the way through a section. A length of one to three minutes or between 24–64 bars would be suitable although there is no minimum or maximum length stated in the specification.

Your choice of piece is very important. Before you choose a piece to sequence, spend some time experimenting with the school equipment to see what instrumental sounds best. Make a list of all the sounds that impress you and a list of the sounds that are particularly poor. When you choose a piece to sequence, it should contain instruments from the 'impressive' list and avoid those from the 'poor' list. It is rare for distorted guitars to sound good on any soundcard or sound module, so avoid choosing a piece that depends on distorted guitar timbres.

Avoid choosing a song to sequence where the vocal part depends more on the delivery and style of the vocal than the melody itself (for example, where the singer has a semi-talking quality to their voice or often bends up to or away from the notes). It is extremely difficult to make a good job of imitating vocal parts like this on a computer.

Glossary

timbre the particular tone colour of an instrument or voice

Glossary

staff the five parallel lines upon which music notation is written

Pay attention to the accuracy of your piece – listen carefully to the original and see how it compares with your sequence, then check the score (or **staff**) view against the score you were working from – does it look the same? There may be some strange rhythms in your on-screen score because you held a note on slightly longer than the given crotchet or played it a tiny bit late – these do not matter as they are points of interpretation. What does matter is the presence of wrong pitches or plainly inaccurate rhythms. In a traditional performance, you would not have the opportunity to go back and correct these unless you re-recorded the whole piece, but with sequencing you are expected to correct any inaccuracies.

After you are satisfied with the accuracy of the piece, you need to think about making it sound as musical as possible. Try to ensure that you include the following:

- dynamics as marked in the original score
- appropriate timbres
- use of controller 7 (main volume) to achieve crescendos and diminuendos over the duration of some long notes
- use of controller 10 (pan) to place the different timbres to the left and right as appropriate. Keep bass instruments and lead instruments central
- reverb (controller 91) as appropriate
- varied articulation of individual notes – you should have accented the notes that need accents, observed staccato markings and so on
- appropriate phrasing – perhaps shortening a duration at the end of a phrase, applying a little rit. if required and so on.

Traditional ensemble performance

Edexcel's definition of an ensemble is where more than one performer is playing at the same time. The following are good examples of an ensemble performance:

- a small chamber group (for example, string quartet, brass quintet)
- the piano accompaniment for any solo instrument
- a vocal duet/trio/quartet and so on with or without backing track
- a rock band
- a large ensemble where the part to be assessed is clear on the recording and is not doubled up by other instruments (for example, 1st trumpet in a concert band).

The following are to be avoided as examples of ensemble performance.

- The solo part in solo and accompaniment (this is essentially the same as a solo).
- Large ensembles where the part to be assessed is not clearly heard or is doubled up by many others on the same part (for example, the soprano part in a large choir).
- A solo piece with a minimal accompaniment added (for example, a solo song with a bongo part added for good measure).

The following are not examples of ensemble performance.

- One soloist and backing track.
- Two vocalists and backing track where both sing the same part or very slightly altered versions of the same line in different places.

The choice of piece for an ensemble is just as important a factor as it is in any performance, as is adequate rehearsal of your chosen piece.

Improvising as part of an ensemble

This option is intended for musicians who are used to playing in styles that usually require an element of improvisation – for example, jazz saxophonists who usually take a solo spot or lead guitarists who usually improvise a solo as part of their band's performances.

The requirements are essentially the same as for solo improvisation except that the actual improvising element does not have to be so long – it is acceptable to present a performance for this option if the improvising element is a sixteen-bar solo in the middle of an otherwise fully notated piece.

You are marked according to your ability to improvise and fit within the ensemble. As with solo improvisation, you are strongly advised to actually practise improvising over the duration of the course, rather than just attempting it once at the end for your recorded submission.

Multi-track recording

This is the music technology option for the ensemble performance. You must record at least three different parts onto a multi-track recorder (drums can only count as one part no matter how many microphones are used to record them).

A multi-track recorder can be either a portastudio device (preferably digital for best sound quality) or a MIDI and audio sequencer such as Sonar, Logic or Cubase.

To obtain the best results, record each part with a separate microphone, either all at once or one at a time.

It is perfectly acceptable for you not to play any of the instruments you are recording – you will be assessed on the final, mixed down recording in this case. Similarly, it is acceptable for you to be the only performer on the recording, overdubbing all the individual parts.

It is also possible for you to sequence some tracks (for example, a rhythm track with some keyboard parts) and record some additional parts – this is counted as a multi-track recording rather than a sequence.

When recording, pay careful attention to the following.
- Ensure the original sound recorded is as clear as possible, with no external noise getting onto the recording (place the microphones carefully).
- The wanted sound should be as loud as possible without distorting – if it is too quiet, then there will be too much noise in the final mix.
- Balance all the tracks carefully so that no instrument is too loud or too quiet, according to how important it is.
- If you have a favourite instrument, be careful you do not make this too loud in the mix.
- Apply effects carefully. Do not overdo them or the recording will sound amateurish. Avoid 'novelty' effects.
- Use some panning to place instruments in the **stereo field.**
- Listen critically to your final recording a few days after you have mixed it. Is there anything you could have done better? If so, mix it again.

Do not try to be too ambitious with your recording – a simple ensemble of between three and six instruments/voices is sufficient. If you try to record too many parts, the mix may become muddy.

Directing an ensemble

This is another option in which you display your musicality in a way other than actually playing the instruments. You are marked on the final performance, so you are expected to have rehearsed the ensemble to the highest standard they are capable of.

Glossary

stereo field the sense of space simulated by reproducing sound through two independent loudspeakers positioned to the left and right of the listener

133

Do not take this option if you intend to show up before the recording and hope that all will be well – you are expected to have led several rehearsals of the group you are directing so that you can build up a rapport with them.

Take notes on what your music teacher does when they direct the school ensembles. What do they ask of the performers? How do they approach a new piece with the ensemble? How do they actually rehearse the piece to make it sound good? How do they communicate with members of the ensemble?

You should take the following into account.
- Treat members of the ensemble with respect.
- Always expect the best from them.
- Insist on everyone observing all markings in the score (dynamics, articulation, tempo markings and so on).
- Listen to as many recordings of the piece you are directing as possible. Which did you like best, and why? How could you get the same results from your ensemble?
- Make all your directions clear, both when you are conducting and when you are speaking to the ensemble.
- Remember that you are in charge.

General points about performance

Your choice of piece is probably the most important part of the whole performance.

Do choose a piece that:
- shows off your abilities
- is within your capabilities of playing well
- allows you to put appropriate expression into the performance
- is a suitable length for your standard of performance
- you enjoy playing (and practising).

Avoid choosing a piece that:
- is too easy
- is pushing your abilities to the very limit or forces you to concentrate so hard on getting the notes right that you cannot think about expression
- is too long
- is too short
- you dislike (you will not be motivated to practise)
- you can only play a part of (rather than the whole piece or whole movement).

Length of pieces

The maximum length of piece for a GCSE performance should be five minutes.

If a piece is very short, it is unlikely you will be able to put enough expression into it to achieve many marks for interpretation.

Difficulty level

A piece can fall into three different levels of difficulty – standard, easier or more difficult. Grade exams cannot be compared directly to levels of difficulty. When you play any piece, it is marked out of 25 and then the mark is adjusted to account for the difficulty of the piece. So, if you played an easy piece really well, scoring 25 out of 25, the mark would be adjusted down to make up for the fact that it is easier. If you played a more difficult piece quite well and scored 20 out of 25, the mark would be adjusted up to make up for the difficulty of the piece. There are only three different options, so there is no level above 'more difficult'. There is no point picking a very tricky piece that is way beyond GCSE standard, because you could pick one that is not as difficult as this but still falls into the 'more difficult' category, still giving you maximum benefit from having your marks scaled up.

Never pick a piece that is too hard for you just to try and force it into the 'more difficult' category – remember that 25 out of 25 at standard difficulty level is still full marks!

Areas of Study

Make sure that one of your performances (either the solo or the ensemble performance) comes from one of the Areas of Study that you used for your compositions. For example, if you composed a piece in AoS 1 (Structure in Western Classical music 1600–1899) and another in AoS 3 (Popular music in context), then make sure that at least one of your pieces comes from at least one of these two areas. You may perform your compositions and submit them as your performance coursework if you wish, as long as they fulfil the other criteria mentioned previously.

Paper 2 – Composing

For this paper, Edexcel requires you to submit the following.

% of GCSE	Requirement	
15%	Composition 1	A composition *based on* one of the AoS or a topic within the AoS (12.5%)
		An 'Understanding the brief' pro forma for composition 1 (2.5%)
15%	Composition 2	A composition based on a *different* AoS than composition 1 (or a topic within a different AoS) (12.5%)
		An 'Understanding the brief' pro forma for composition 2 (2.5%)

Both pieces need to be recorded onto a CD/MD or cassette. You need to submit a copy of the score for your composition or an alternative notation that would allow another musician to perform your piece. The recording can be either computer generated or performed by live musicians.

What does 'based on' mean?

The music you compose must be based on work you have studied for your Listening and Appraising exam. This means that each piece must show influences from one of the AoS. You can choose to base your piece on the title of the AoS itself (for example, Popular music in context) or you can be more specific, basing it on one of the topic titles within that AoS (for example, Dance music 1985–present day).

It is necessary to show how you have been influenced by the AoS or topic title, so keep a log of your ideas detailing how you have gradually developed them. This way, when it comes to filling out the 'Understanding the brief' pro forma, you can demonstrate how your work links to the original concept. It is especially important to do this if the influences are not immediately obvious.

You could also combine topics from different areas of study. For example, you could use some ideas from Indian **raga** in a dance music piece or you could write an **expressionist** piece in **rondo** form.

Glossary

expressionist used to describe the highly emotional output of many artists, writers and composers at the start of the 20th century

raga improvised music in several contrasting sections, based on a series of notes from a particular rag

rondo classical form comprising a series of rondo sections interspersed with contrasting episodes. The simple rondo was structured as ABACA, where A = the rondo theme and B and C = the episodes

What is a brief?

Before you begin your piece, you should have a brief. A brief is a set of criteria or instructions you must fulfil for your piece to be successful. If your brief says you are going to write a **ternary** form piece for string quartet for performance at your sister's wedding, and you write a death metal piece for eight heavily distorted guitars and bongos in no particular form, you have not fulfilled your brief.

Understanding the brief

'Understanding the brief' pro formas are worth a total of 5% of your GCSE. If filled in thoughtfully, you could have 5% of your GCSE sewn up before you begin anything else!

The first step to scoring this 5% is to keep a good log throughout the composition process. This should include the following:

- Details of any decisions you have made regarding structure and instrumentation (and reasons for these decisions).
- Any ideas you had for developing your themes.
- Changes you made after listening to your piece (at any stage of its development) and the reasons why you made the changes – this is called 'making critical judgements'.
- Any other points of interest.

After you have completed your piece and made any final adjustments, you can refer back to your log and use the information for the official Edexcel form. You do not have to use musical vocabulary in your log – use any language you want to, as long as you will understand it later.

Before you write on the official form, attempt it in rough draft. Summarize your log, keeping the important points and leaving out the tiny details that have no bearing on the whole piece. At this point, you must include appropriate musical vocabulary. Failure to do so will stop you from getting the top marks available.

Refer to how you fulfilled the brief, making sure you do not leave out any points listed in the brief. If you can do this while summarizing your log, so much the better.

If your piece is based on a story (it is programmatic), you may include this in the pro forma, but summarize the story and always put it in its musical context (for example, the flute arpeggios represent the waterfall). Just telling the story is insufficient – you must always link your story to the music.

Glossary

ternary (ABA) a three part form. The first and last sections are identical or similar. The middle section (B) provides a contrast

What makes a good composition?

There are some general points that examiners look for in
all pieces:
- development of ideas (melodies, riffs, themes, rhythms)
- how well the piece has fulfilled the brief
- how well the resources (instruments, vocals, sound
  sources) have been used
- a clear and well-balanced structure appropriate to the style.

Use of resources

When you write for an instrument, you should use more than
just one octave of its range. If you are writing for your own
instrument, look at what other composers have done in pieces
you have played. How did they use the full potential of the
instrument?

Do not feel limited by what you can play yourself – few, if any,
of the great composers could play all the instruments they
ever wrote for, they just understood the capabilities of the
instruments and had some idea of what they would sound like.

Are there any particular techniques you should be aware of
when writing for your chosen instrument (for example, arco
or pizzicato for strings)? Check with someone you know who
plays the instrument whether what you have written is possible
to play, or if you have forgotten something important.

Does the instrumental combination work well together? Do
you make good use of all the instruments? Is everything you
have written within the instrument's range?

Structure

Your piece should have a clear and well-balanced structure
appropriate to the style. This may be something less obvious
than ternary form if you are writing a minimalist piece. A
structure appropriate to minimalism may consist of a gradual
build up with a sudden change to a different combination of
rhythmic motifs, which build up in turn. Similarly, dance music
may have a structure based on repetition and the gradual build
up of texture within a verse/chorus structure. Most styles will
have a preferred set of forms that are used commonly by the
main composers in the style.

Music is unsuccessful if the composer has not given some thought to structure. Even the electronic music of Stockhausen, which has no climaxes or build ups as we would expect in most music, is in a form he called 'moment form'. Most music has a series of highs and lows, with clearly defined sections. Avoid directionless waffle.

Melody, harmony, accompaniment, texture, rhythm, tempo, dynamics

How you use the above depends on the style in which you are writing. Some pieces may have no melody or harmony at all while others depend on them almost to the exclusion of everything else. Ensure you have given some thought to each of the above, even if only to decide that it does not apply to your piece. Ensure that your piece contains enough variety through use of the different musical elements, but it still holds together as a unified whole.

Time management

Coursework can be completed at any time over the duration of your course. Each time your teacher sets you a performing or composition assignment, you have the opportunity to complete part of your course, reducing any pressure you are likely to face when the exams themselves come around. Take these opportunities seriously and approach each task as if it is the piece of work you are going to hand in to the moderator.

Understanding music

In this topic you will learn about:

- staff, clefs, note names, tones and semitones, flats and sharps, note values, dotted notes and rests
- time signatures and key signatures
- scales
- degrees of the scale and intervals
- simple harmony – triads and inversions, the primary triads, the secondary triads and cadences
- musical devices and the elements of music.

This chapter is intended for reference, for you to dip into during your GCSE course.

Staff and clefs

The two most common **clefs** that you will come across are:
- the **treble (or G) clef**
- the **bass (or F) clef**.

Two other clefs that you may come across are:
- the **alto C clef**
- the **tenor C clef**.

The clefs are written on a five-line **staff** (or **stave**).

The four clefs:

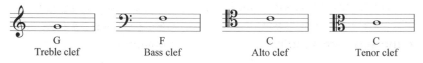

| G | F | C | C |
| Treble clef | Bass clef | Alto clef | Tenor clef |

The instruments that use these different clefs depend on their pitch range.
- Treble clef instruments include the piccolo, flute, clarinet, oboe, trumpet (cornet), French horn, saxophone, violin, recorder, soprano and alto voices.
- Bass clef instruments include the bassoon, tuba, cello, double bass and bass voice.
- The alto C clef is mainly used for the viola.
- The tenor C clef is used in conjunction with the bass clef for the high notes on the bassoon, trombone, cello and double bass.

Glossary

alto C clef the clef used mainly by the viola

bass or 'F' clef clef that fixes the note F on the fourth line of the stave

clef French for key, clefs fix a particular note on the stave

staff/stave the five parallel lines upon which music notation is written

tenor C clef used in conjunction with the bass clef for high notes on the bassoon, trombone, cello, and double bass

treble (or G clef) this fixes the note G on the second line of the stave. The treble clef is used for high pitched instruments/ voices

Note names

The musical language uses the letter names **A**, **B**, **C**, **D**, **E**, **F** and **G**, then starts again with **A**. The distance between one A and the next A is eight notes. This is called an **octave** (oct = 8). The following extract shows the notes on the lines and spaces of the treble and bass clefs.

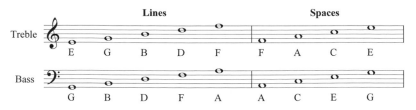

Tones and semitones, flats and sharps

The distance between two notes is called a **tone**. The two exceptions to this are between the notes E to F and B to C. In these cases, the distance between the notes is only a **semitone**. You can see this in the picture of a keyboard opposite.

If we raise a note by a semitone, we sharpen the note. If we lower a note by a semitone, we flatten it.

As the distance between the notes E to F and B to C is a semitone already, if we sharpen the note E, it becomes E#, which is also the note F. In the same way, F♭ is also E, B# is C, and C♭ is B.

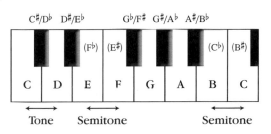

Note values

The different note values all stem from the longest note, called the **breve**, lasting for eight beats. The diagram below shows the division of the breve to include the **semibreve**, minim, crotchet, quaver and semiquaver.

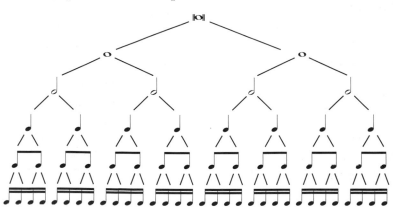

Breve	8 beats x 1
Semibreve	4 beats x 2
Minim	2 beats x 4
Crotchet	1 beat x 8
Quaver	$\frac{1}{2}$ beat x 16
Semiquaver	$\frac{1}{4}$ beat x 32

Dotted notes

The effect of placing a dot after a note increases the length of the original note by half as much again (that is, an extra 50 per cent).

Therefore:

- a dotted crotchet = a crotchet (one beat) plus half the value of the original note (half a beat) equals one-and-a-half beats

$$\text{♩.} = \text{♩} + \text{♪}$$

- a dotted minim = a minim (two beats) plus half the value of the original note (one beat) equals three beats

$$\text{𝅗𝅥.} = \text{𝅗𝅥} + \text{♩}$$

- a dotted quaver = a quaver (half a beat) plus half the value of the original note (quarter of a beat) equals three-quarters of a beat.

$$\text{♪.} = \text{♪} + \text{♬}$$

Rests

Rests that provide silence in music are just as important as sound created by notes. The common rests are:

BREVE	SEMIBREVE	MINIM	CROTCHET	QUAVER	SEMIQUAVER	DEMISEMIQUAVER

A dotted rest has the same effect as a dotted note – for example, a dotted crotchet rest equals a crotchet (one beat) plus half again, that is, a quaver (half a beat) equals one-and-a-half beats.

Time signatures

The two figures at the start of a piece of music are called the **time signature**. The top figure is the number of beats in each bar.

The bottom figure is like a code to represent the type of beat – for example, a 4 represents the crotchet. Therefore 4/4 means there are four crotchet beats in each bar, that is:

4 = number of beats
4 = type of beat

The important thing is to know what the bottom figure represents. The common ones are:

2 = minim   4 = crotchet   8 = quaver   16 = semiquaver.

Therefore, a time signature of 6/8 means that there are six quaver beats in a bar.

Glossary

time signature the two numbers at the beginning of a piece of music. The top number refers to the number of beats per bar and the bottom figure indicates the type of beat

Simple and compound time signatures

Time signatures where the beat can be divided into two are **simple time signatures**. Time signatures where the beat can be divided into three are **compound time signatures**.

$$\frac{2}{4} = \; \flat \quad \flat \quad = \quad \text{♩♩} \quad \text{♩♩}$$

The beat is divided into two, so it is simple time.
As there are two beats in each bar, it is simple duple time.
So 3/4 = simple triple and 4/4 = simple quadruple.

$$\frac{6}{8} = \; \flat. \quad \flat. \quad = \quad \text{♪♪♪} \quad \text{♪♪♪}$$

The beat is divided into three, so it is compound time.
As there are two beats in each bar, it is compound duple.
So 9/8 = compound triple and 12/8 = compound quadruple.

Key signatures

Music can be written in a variety of different keys, both **major** and **minor**. Each major key has its own related minor key with the same key signature – for example, C major has A minor as its relative minor.

The following diagram shows you all the major and minor keys. Each key is five notes apart, and this is called the circle of fifths because eventually you arrive back at the start. The order of sharps proceeds in a clockwise direction (C, G, D and so on) and the flats in an anticlockwise direction from C (C, F, B♭ and so on). This diagram will provide a useful reference chart for you.

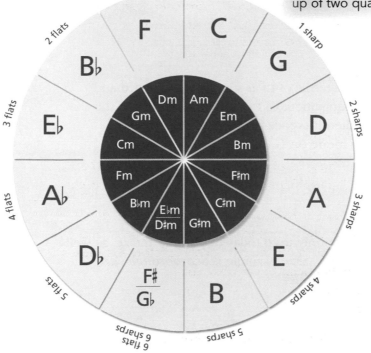

Order of sharps and flats.

Scales

There are many types of scales and you should have an understanding of:

- **modes**
- minor
- chromatic
- major
- pentatonic
- whole-tone scales.

Modes

Modes came into use a long time before the major/minor scales. These modes are easy to understand at the piano or keyboard. They are basically constructed of eight consecutive notes but only using the white keys – for example, take the notes D to D (that is, D, E, F, G, A, B, C and D). This is a mode called the dorian mode and each of these modes has a different name, as can be seen below.

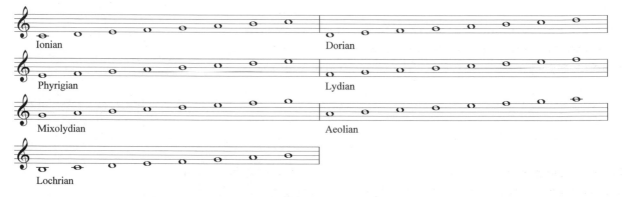

The modes differ in terms of their sound when played and in terms of the arrangement of tones and semitones in the pattern. Look at the difference between the mode on A (aeolian) and the mode on G (mixolydian):

Aeolian	Mixolydian
A – B – C – D – E – F – G – A	G – A – B – C – D – E – F – G
t s t t s t t	t t s t t s t

Modes are still commonly used today in popular music, as well as in British folk music. One example is *Scarborough Fair*, written in the dorian mode.

Major scales

The major scales are constructed of eight notes that all follow the same pattern of tones and semitones, in the set sequence:

tone, tone, semitone, tone, tone, tone, semitone.

The following music shows how this works with C major.

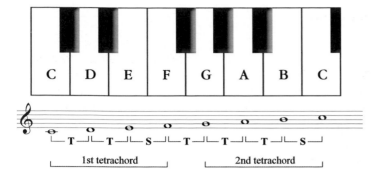

Minor scales

There are two forms of minor scales: **harmonic** and **melodic**.

The harmonic minor scale is the same ascending and descending and has a semitone between the seventh and eighth notes, which gives the interval of a tone-and-a-half between notes 6 and 7. This gives these forms of minor keys their characteristic 'eastern' sound. Look at A minor (harmonic) as an example:

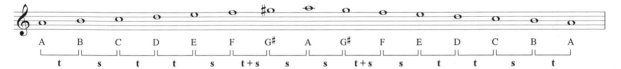

The melodic minor scales are a little more complex in that they have different versions ascending and descending. In simple terms, the sixth and seventh degrees are raised by a semitone on the way up and then flattened on the way down.

Using the previous example of A minor, here are the basic notes:

Now we add the sharpened sixth and seventh, and then flatten these two notes on the way down. A sharp flattened by a semitone becomes a natural. Likewise, a flat sharpened becomes a natural.

Pentatonic scales

'Pente' means 'five'. Pentatonic scales are built up using the first, second, third, fifth and sixth notes of the scale. They are commonly used in folk tunes and other melodies such as the hymn tune *Amazing Grace*.

In C major, these notes would be:

C   D   E   G   A

Another easy way to compose using just pentatonic notes is to use only the black keys on the keyboard, G♭, A♭, B♭, D♭ and E♭.

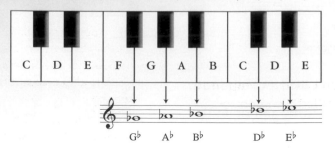

G♭   A♭   B♭   D♭   E♭

Chromatic scales

The word 'chromatic' means 'colour' and is a scale that comprises the twelve semitones within an octave, that is:

C   C♯   D   D♯   E   F   F♯   G   G♯   A   A♯   B   C

Whole-tone scales

These scales were popular with the twentieth-century impressionist composers such as Achille-Claude Debussy (1862–1918) and Maurice Ravel (1875–1937) and, as the name suggests, they are made up of a sequence of tones:

C   D   E   F♯   G♯   A♯   (C)

Degrees of the scale

The eight notes in a scale have specific technical names assigned to them. The three most important are those based on the first, fourth and fifth degrees. Roman numerals are used to describe the degrees of the scale:

- I = tonic
- IV = subdominant
- V = dominant.

However, it is useful to know all eight, as printed below.

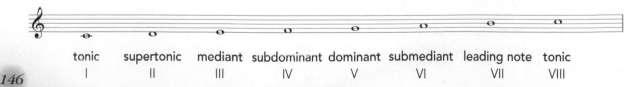

tonic	supertonic	mediant	subdominant	dominant	submediant	leading note	tonic
I	II	III	IV	V	VI	VII	VIII

Intervals

The distance between any two notes is called the **interval**. To work out the number of the interval, simply count up from the lowest note (count this note as 1) to the next note, including lines and spaces. See the extract below:

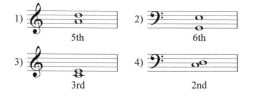

An interval greater than an octave is often called a **compound interval**. Therefore a ninth can also be called a compound second.

This gives you the basic numeric description of the interval, but you also need to know what is called the quality of the interval – that is, major, minor, **perfect**, **augmented** or **diminished**.

If you imagine the bottom note to be the key note of the scale (in this case, the note is C, so we are in C major), then you can work out the following intervals.

| Maj | Maj | Perf. | Perf. | Maj | Maj | Maj (or perfect octave) |
| 2nd | 3rd | 4th | 5th | 6th | 7th | 8th |

Simple harmony

Triads

A **chord** is made up of at least two notes sounded simultaneously together. A **triad** is a three-note chord, the prefix 'tri' meaning 'three'.

The basic triad uses a root note plus a third above this and a note a fifth above the root note, as shown in the C major triad below. There are triads on each degree of the scale, too.

C major

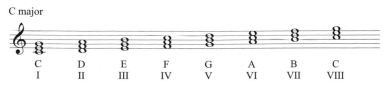

Triads can also be built on notes from minor scales, as shown in the example below in the key of A minor.

A minor

Glossary

augmented to make larger by a semitone, as in an augmented interval

chord the simultaneous sounding together of two or more notes

compound interval an interval larger than an octave. For example a ninth is also a compound second

diminished to make smaller by a semitone

interval distance between any two notes

Glossary

perfect (i) a perfect interval, such as the 4th, 5th and 8th (ii) a type of cadence. Chord V followed by chord I. A conclusive cadence, sometimes referred to as a full close

triad a three note chord ('Tri' means three)

Inversions

Look back at the C major triad given as chord I in C major on page 147. This is in **root position** because the root of the chord (C) is in the bass.

To 'invert' the chord, we can do two things:
* have the third in the bass – this is called **first inversion**
* have the fifth in the bass – this is called **second inversion**.

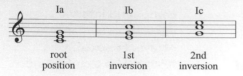

To tell the chords apart, root position chord I is written as Ia, first inversion is Ib and second inversion is Ic.

The primary triads

Primary triads form the basis of all harmony and are therefore of primary importance. They comprise the three chords of I, IV and V in every key.

These primary triads provide the basic 'colour' of the harmony. By using just these three chords, we can harmonize every note in the key of C major. The twelve-bar blues and reggae songs were often based solely on these three chords, and many popular songs too only use a limited number of chords.

The primary triads in C major and C minor are shown below.

The secondary triads

The secondary triads are chords II and VI, and in a major key these are both minor chords. In C major, for example, this would be a chord of D minor (II) and A minor (VI). In a minor key, chord II is diminished and chord VI is major. The secondary triads in C major and C minor are shown below.

Cadences

Cadences are a type of musical punctuation. There are four common types of cadences that you need to know. Each cadence consists of two chords only and there are four common types that you need to know.

- The **perfect cadence** (or full close) = chords V–I. This is like a full stop as it is conclusive and is often used to end a passage or section of music.
- The **imperfect cadence** (or half close) = chords I–V, or II–V or IV–V (in fact, anything–V). This is the comma. It ends on the dominant chord, so we are aware that the musical sentence is incomplete and there will be more to come.
- The **plagal cadence** (or the 'amen cadence') = chords IV–I. This is a gentler version of a perfect cadence. Chord IV is softer than the strong dominant chord and this cadence has associations with sacred music of the church, hence the reference to the 'amen' cadence.
- The **interrupted cadence** = chords V–VI. The interrupted cadence literally 'interrupts' a perfect cadence. The listener is expecting chord I after chord V, but this is followed by chord VI, effectively like a semicolon, because the music has more to add before concluding its musical sentence.

The four cadences written out in the key of C major and C minor in four-part harmony set for a four-part SATB choir (soprano, alto, tenor and bass) are shown below:

Glossary

imperfect cadence a cadence ending on chord V which sounds incomplete. Usually preceded by chord I, II, or IV

interrupted cadence most commonly comprises chord 5 followed by chord 6. So called because the expected perfect cadence V-I has been interrupted by the unexpected chord 6

perfect cadence chord V followed by chord I

plagal cadence chord IV followed by chord I – the 'Amen Cadence' or English cadence

a) Perfect cadence

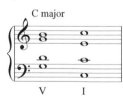

b) Plagal cadence

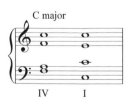

c) Imperfect cadence

d) Interrupted cadence

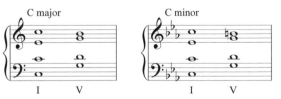
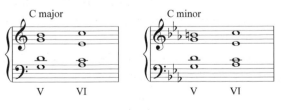

Musical devices

Many devices are used in music. Here are some of the most common you will come across.

Drone

This usually features the sustained tonic and dominant notes together, although the two notes can alternate. It is commonly a feature of the harmony and will be used to support a melody. Bagpipes use this principle of a drone bass with a melody played on the chanter.

Pedal

A sustained note, usually dominant or tonic, hence called a tonic pedal or a dominant pedal. If the sustained note is the lowest part in the musical texture, it is called the **pedal**. If the sustained note is in the middle of a texture, it is called an **inner pedal**, and if it appears as the highest part, it is called an **inverted pedal**.

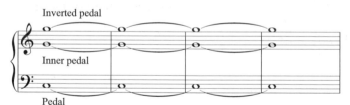

Glossary

inner pedal a sustained note in the middle of the musical texture

inverted pedal a sustained note at the top of the musical texture

pedal a sustained note usually in the lowest bass part

Alberti bass

This is a common type of figuration used as an accompaniment. It was invented by the composer Domenico Alberti (1710–1740) during the Classical era and has been extensively used since.

Arpeggio/broken chords

These are two useful types of accompaniment (or figuration) that can easily be employed in a passage of music.

Ostinato/riff

An ostinato (or 'riff', as it is called in popular and jazz music) is simply a short repeated phrase. An ostinato can be a repeated rhythm, melody or chord sequence. Quite often, the ostinato will be a combination of these features. This well-known football chant is an example of a rhythmic ostinato.

repeat

The elements of music

This final section looks at the key elements of music that you will be expected to understand and recognize by the end of your GCSE course. These are the key elements of:

- pitch
- duration
- dynamics
- tempo
- timbre
- texture
- structure.

Pitch

Pitch refers to how high or low the music sounds at any particular point. Pitch can include reference to melody and harmony, and involves all types of notation, including conventional staff notation, non-standard and graphic score notations.

Glossary

pitch how high or low a note(s) sounds

The associated musical vocabulary that you need to be familiar with is summarized below.

Pitch	Melody	Harmony and tonality	Notation
Pitch names	Step	Consonant	Staff notation
Sharp, flat	Leap	Dissonant	Treble and bass
Octave	Scalic	Major	Stave (staff)
Intervals	Interval	Minor	Bar/double bar lines
Range	Chromatic	Modal	Key and time signatures
Register	Glissando	Atonal	Note values
Diatonic key		Cadences	Phrase
Tonic		Modulation	Articulation mark
Subdominant		Transpose	Dynamic signs
Dominant		Pedal	Ornament signs
Pentatonic		Drone	Graphic score
Raga		Chord pattern	Non-standard notation
Note row		Arpeggio/broken chords	Three-line staves
			Oral tradition

Duration

This refers to the length of musical sounds. You need to know the following terms:

- note values – for example, crotchets, semiquavers and so on
- pulse/beat
- triplet
- dotted rhythm
- phrase length and shape
- phrase structure.

Dynamics

In your listening exam, you will be asked to comment on the dynamics in an extract and to describe how dynamics change, including crescendos and diminuendos. The articulation of the music (how it is played) is often linked to dynamics.

Dynamics		Articulation
Fortissimo	Crescendo	Legato (smooth)
Forte	Diminuendo	Staccato (short and detached)
Mezzo forte	Subito (suddenly)	Tremolo (wavering)
Mezzo piano	Accent/sforzando	
Piano/pianissimo		Pizzacato

Tempo

The speed or **tempo** of the music is expressed mainly in Italian terms and you need to know the following basic terms:

Glossary

tempo speed of the music

Tempo	Tempo changes
Adagio – slow	Accelerando – getting faster
Largo – slow and broad	Ritardando/rallentando – slowing down
Andante – at a walking pace (medium tempo)	Allargando – broadening out
Allegro – fast	Rubato – 'robbed' time, not in strict tempo
Vivace – fast and lively	Silence
Presto – very fast	Pause

Timbre

The **timbre** of music means the tone quality of the sound and the difference between sounds – for example, the timbre of a trumpet is quite different from the timbre of a flute. Timbre depends on the materials with which an instrument is made, the way it is played and how the sound is produced.

You will need to be able to identify changes in musical timbre and also to be able to recognize the sounds of individual orchestral instruments, as well as the sounds of various instrumental ensembles such as the sound of a string quartet or a jazz band.

Glossary

timbre particular tone colour of an instrument or voice

Vocal sounds	Instrumental sounds	Ensembles
Soprano/treble	Brass instruments	Orchestra
Alto	Percussion	Chamber orchestra
Tenor	Strings	Wind band
Bass	Woodwind	Brass band
Falsetto	Electric instruments	Pop band, rock band
Choir	Keyboard instruments	Indian/African ensemble
Chorus	Indian instruments:	Quintets/quartets/trios/duets
A cappella	sitar/sarod/sarangai/	
Backing vocals	tambura/tabla	
	African instruments:	
	djembe/talking drums/agogo	
	bells/master drummer/kora/mbira/	

Texture

Texture describes two different but related elements of music.

1 The number and movement of musical parts and how this can vary during the course of a piece or extract. Words to describe this aspect of texture include:
   - number of parts
   - tutti – all playing
   - solo line – one part (called monophonic)
   - descant/counter melody – a second melody added to the texture
   - sparse texture – just a few musical parts or lines present (for example, a solo flute accompanied by a cello)
   - dense texture – a texture that is 'busy' and is characterized by many instruments or different parts
   - varied texture – most musical textures will fall into this category and will change frequently during a piece of music in order to provide both variety and interest.

Glossary

texture the number of parts in a piece of music and how they relate to one another. There are several distinct types. See **homophony**, **polyphony**, **monophony**, and **heterophony**

2 A particular type of established and recognized texture.

- **Monophonic** – literally means just 'one sound'. A single musical line, but can be sung or played by many people.
- **Homophonic** – literally means 'same sounds'. Melody and accompaniment style. Parts move roughly together. This is the most common type of musical texture.
- **Polyphonic** – literally means 'many sounds'. Two or more parts playing a melody and entering the texture individually to create a contrapuntal texture. Common in Renaissance vocal music.
- **Heterophonic** – literally means a 'difference of sounds'. Two or more parts play a melody together but with some slight differences in pitch. This is common in Eastern musical traditions where music is learnt and played by ear (oral tradition).

Structure

All of the musical elements discussed so far can be found within the musical structure or form. The structures that you will need to know are the structures that you have studied in your topics from the four Areas of Study. This section also includes common musical devices that occur within musical structures.

Structure	Musical devices
Ground bass and variations	Repetition/sequence
Rondo/ritornello	Ostinato/riffs
Ternary form	Imitation/canon
Minuet and trio	Motific development
Song verse/chorus structure	Introduction
Indian raga structure	Coda
Call and response	Link
Aleatoric/chance	

Glossary

heterophonic musical texture in which several parts play the same melodic part but with slight differences in pitch. Common in Turkish music, Indonesian gamelan music and Japanese music

homophonic common musical texture comprising a melody part and some form of accompaniment

monophonic musical texture of a single melodic line with no accompaniment

polyphonic a texture featuring two or more parts, each having a melody line and sounding together. Creates a multilayered texture

Glossary

4-to-the-floor very prominent, regular bass drum played on each beat of a 4/4 bar

affection refers to the prevailing mood or emotion expressed in the music of the Baroque era

alap the opening unmetered and improvised section of an Indian raga

aleatoric music in which some aspects of composition or realisation are left to chance

alto clef the clef used mainly by the viola

analogue synth synthesiser which uses voltage controlled oscillators, filters and amplifiers in conjunction with envelope generators, low frequency oscillators and other analogue circuitry to create and manipulate waveforms which are heard via a loudspeaker

anthem a song that has achieved a certain longevity due to its popularity and is often instantly recognisable by its distinctive introduction

arpeggio the sounding of the tones of a chord in rapid succession rather than simultaneously

atonal music which is not in any key

attack the part of a sound that occurs immediately after it is sounded. The speed of the attack determines how quickly a note 'speaks': a sound which gradually fades in has a slow attack, but a sound which is very sudden has a fast attack

augmented to make larger by a semitone, as in an augmented interval

bandish last section of a vocal raga performance. This is a 'fixed composition' in the form of a song

bansuri an Indian flute without keys

bass or 'F' clef clef that fixes the note F on the fourth line of the stave

basso continuo literally 'a continuous bass part', usually figured to show the chords to be played by the keyboard player (harpsichord or organ). The bass line would be played by the cello (or bassoon)

basso ostinato a repeated bass melody, usually of between two to four bars duration

bhang the hemp crop harvested by Punjabi peasant farmer workers that led to the name of their folk music called Bhangra

bols in a tala, these are the independent rhythm parts that go against the main beat of the cycle creating exciting syncopations

breakbeats drum patterns, often high tempo, which include a significant amount of syncopation and polyrhythms

breve literally 'a breath' – a long note of eight crotchet beats duration

brimintingo in African Kora music, these are simple repetitive rhythms and improvisations on the melody (kumbengo)

Burlesque a parody or humorous piece

cadence two chords at the end of a musical phrase. Four main types: perfect, imperfect, interrupted and plagal

call and response simple form involving a solo (call) followed by a group answering phrase (response)

chaal the basic eight beat rhythmic cycle used in Bhangra

chaconne and passacaglia similar forms consisting of a set of continuous variations based on a ground bass. Unlike ground bass form itself, the ground can appear in different parts of the musical texture

chromaticism notes used that are foreign to the key of the music. For example, sharps and flats in the key of c major would be chromatic notes

clefs French for key, clefs fix a particular note on the stave

coda final short section of a piece of music literally meaning 'tail piece'

col legno in string music, this means to be played with the wood of the bow

compound interval an interval larger than an octave. For example a ninth is also a compound second

compound time signature a time signature where the beat is subdivided into groups of three, as in 6/8 which has two dotted crotchet beats, each of which comprises three quavers

concertante name given to the solo or solo group in a Baroque concerto grosso

concerto piece for a solo instrument and orchestra. The form has three movements, usually fast-slow-fast

cross rhythms rhythms that literally cross the usual pattern of accented and unaccented beats creating irregular accents and syncopated effects. Groupings of notes can go over barlines too

da capo al fine instruction placed at the end of a piece, meaning 'go back to the beginning' (da capo = 'from the head') and end at the word 'fine'.

decay the last part of a sound; the speed of the decay determines how long it takes for the sound to fade away

delay an effect, similar to echo, involving the repetition of a sound at a set time interval for a given number of repeats, with each repeat quieter than the one before

dhol large double-headed barrel drum, used in the Punjabi region of India in performances of Bhangra

diatonic notes belonging to or literally 'of the key' In diatonic harmony, these are chords in the key of the music

diminished to make smaller by a semitone

divertimento 18th century suite of movements of light music for a small number of players (Italian for 'entertainment')

djembe goblet-shaped drum from West Africa

dominant fifth note of the scale or key – the strongest note after the tonic

donno hourglass shaped 'talking drum' held under the arm and played with the hand. This drum can play several different pitches by stretching the skin of the drum head

drone a sustained sound

dundun double-headed drum played with sticks. There are several different sizes of instrument

enharmonic different ways of 'spelling' the same pitch, for example Bb and A#. One 'spelling' will make more harmonic sense than the other in tonal music, but the two are often interchangeable in atonal or highly chromatic music

environmental noise background noise, such as that made by traffic outside an auditorium or the humming of electrical equipment

episodes a contrasting musical section (for example in ritornello and rondo forms)

expressionist term used to describe the highly emotional output of many artists, writers and composers at the start of the 20th century

extravaganzas stage shows containing a variety of acts

figured bass a numbered bass part. The figures indicate the chords to be played by the keyboard player

first inversion a chord with the third in the bass. A chord of c major (c-e-g-) in first inversion would be **e**-g-c

flanger effect produced by feeding a percentage of a delayed sound source back into the original – the aural effect is a sweeping or 'swooshing' sound

gat the final section of an instrumental raga performance. The music in this section is not improvised but features a 'fixed composition' which is performcd with some additional improvised embellishments

gharana in Indian music, the extended musical family in which pupils learn from a master

graphic score a visual representation of a piece of music which does not need to include any traditional form of musical notation. Often a significant amount of interpretation is required by the performer in order to realise the score

griot African Music. In Mandika society, from the fifteenth century, this was a school of musicians who preserved the stories from its history through songs accompanied on the Kora

ground bass a Baroque form in which a bass melody called the 'ground' is played continuously to a set of variations in the other instrumental or vocal parts

grunge genre of rock music from the North West of the USA inspired by indie music, punk and thrash metal and at its most popular during the late 1980s and early 1990

harmonic relates to the harmony parts.

heterophonic musical texture in which several parts play the same melodic part but with slight differences in pitch. Common in Turkish music, Indonesian gamelan music and Japanese music

homophonic common musical texture comprising a melody part and some form of accompaniment

imperfect cadence a cadence ending on chord V which sounds incomplete. Usually preceeded by chord I, II, or IV

impressionist term used to describe the paintings of Monet, Pissarro and others, which was later applied to the music of Debussy, Ravel and other composers who used musical colour in a way comparable to the painters

improvise make up music spontaneously.

indeterminacy music in which some or all aspects of composition and realisation are left to chance

Indie music music distributed by means other than the large record and distribution companies. The smaller record labels who use alternative distribution methods are known as 'independent labels' and artists who record with these labels are known as 'independent' or 'indie' artists

inner pedal a sustained note in the middle of the musical texture.

interrupted cadence most commonly comprises chord 5 followed by chord 6. So called because the expected perfect cadence V-I has been interrupted by the unexpected chord 6

interval distance between any two notes.

inversion process involving turning a part upside down, so that a mirror image is created to the original

inverted pedal a sustained note at the top of the musical texture

isicathamiya traditional vocal music of the Zulus of South Africa

jhala the third section of a raga performance. Features include a lively tempo and virtuoso display of improvisatory skills. The highlight or climax of the whole piece is in this section

jhor the second section in a typical raga performance. In medium tempo featuring improvisation by the soloist

kumbengo the melody line in African Kora music

kushaura the lead melody part in Mbira music

kutsinhira the second intertwining melody to the main **Kushaura** melody in Mbira music

leading note The seventh degree of the scale

linear music that is conceived in terms of lines of melody rather than in chords or harmony

major western tonal music in bright sounding keys. A major key has four semitones between the first and third notes (C-E)

matras individual beats in a rhythmic cyclc

mediant the third degree of the scale

meend (or mind) in Indian music, the sliding effects between notes

melodic refers to the melody line

melodrama drama in which spoken lines are punctuated by music

membranophones category of instruments that have a drum skin (membrane)

minor western tonal music in solemn sounding keys. A minor key has three semitones between the first and third notes (C-Eb)

minstrelsy form of entertainment, popular in the 1800s, in which white actors would be made up in 'blackface' to imitate black slaves and poke fun at the rich and powerful

minuet and trio a ternary form structure, performed as minuet-trio-minuet. The minuet is a stately dance in triple time and the contrasting middle section (trio) usually features a reduction in instrumental parts. Often used as the third movement in a classical symphony

modes precursors of modern scales. There are seven different modes, each with a different series of tones and semitones

monophonic musical texture of a single melodic line with no accompaniment

motifs short melodic or rhythmic ideas used as a basis for manipulation and development in a musical composition

note addition a method of developing cells in minimalist music by gradually adding notes to the original cell

note subtraction a method of developing cells in minimalist music by gradually taking notes away from the original cell

obbligato prominent solo part in the musical texture

octave the interval of eight notes, eg C to C eight notes higher

ondes martenot an early synthesiser with a ribbon controller in addition to the keyboard, facilitating glissandi and intervals of less than a semitone

opéra-bouffe a light opera, often with spoken dialogue and some comical content

operetta light opera

oral tradition music that is learnt by listening and repeating. A tradition of passing music down orally from one generation to another. The music is not normally written down in traditional notation.

oratorio large scale musical setting for chorus, soloists and orchestra of a biblical text. Designed for concert performance. The most famous example is the oratorio 'Messiah' by G.F Handel

ostinato/ostinati a repeated rhythm, melody or chord pattern. In popular musical styles, these are called **riffs**

overture an opening instrumental piece, usually played before an opera or musical. Sets the scene and often features some of the main themes to be heard later in the main work

pan spreading a signal in the stereo field by feeding different levels of the sound to the left and right speakers

pedal a sustained note usually in the lowest bass part. In the middle of a musical texture it is called an **inner pedal** and if at the top, an **inverted pedal**

perfect (i) a perfect interval, such as the 4th, 5th and 8th; (ii) a type of **cadence**: chord V followed by chord I

perfect cadence chord V followed by chord I.

phasing when two or more versions of a sound or musical motif are played simultaneously but slightly out of synchronisation. Often this is used as a development technique in minimalism where the start points of the motifs will gradually converge after a period of time

pitch how high or low a note(s) sounds

plagal cadence chord IV followed by chord I – the 'Amen Cadence' or English cadence

polyphonic see polyphony

polyphony a texture featuring two or more parts, each having a melody line and sounding together. Creates a multilayered texture

polyrhythmic texture a texture made up of many different rhythms

polyrhythm two or more different rhythms played together

prime row (P$_0$) the musical material on which a piece of serial music is based, normally consisting of the 12 notes of the chromatic scale in an order set by the composer (also known as the series, the note row or the tone row)

raga improvised music in several contrasting sections, based on a series of notes from a particular rag

rasa mood created by the sounds of the pitches in a particular rag

repetition the restatement of a section of music. This might be just a few notes or a whole section of music

retrograde (R$_0$) a method of developing a series by reversing the order in which the pitches are heard

retrograde inversion (RI$_0$) a method of developing a series by reversing the order in which the pitches of the inverted series are heard

reverb the effect produced when a sound is reflected by the surrounding surfaces – this natural effect is imitated by electronic devices used in recording studios to give the impression of space or depth

ritornello Baroque 'rondo' form featuring alternating sections of the ritornello theme and contrasting episodes. The episodes were often solo sections in a reduced instrumental texture

rondo classical form comprising a series of rondo sections interspersed with contrasting episodes. The simple rondo was structured as ABACA, where A = the rondo theme and B and C = the episodes

root position chord with the root in the bass. In the case of a chord of c major, this would be c-e-g

sam in Indian music, the first beat of the rhythmic cycle (tala)

samplers devices used to capture and manipulate a sound, often by changing its pitch or by playing selected snippets of the original

scat singing type of jazz singing style featuring improvised syllables in complex rhythm patterns

scratch a sound produced by manually spinning a vinyl disk at a different speed than originally intended (backwards or forwards) while the needle is in contact with the disk

scherzo and trio a ternary (ABA) structure, in which the scherzo section is repeated. The scherzo is a lively and fast movement (scherzo is Italian for 'joke'), while the contrasting trio section has a reduced orchestration and/or number of parts

second inversion a chord with the fifth in the bass. A chord of c major (c-e-g) in second inversion would be **g**-c-e

semibreve long note lasting for four crotchet beats.

semitone half a tone. The distance between a white note and an adjacent black note on a keyboard

serialism a compositional technique invented by Arnold Schoenberg and used by many composers of the 20th century

shenai a double reed Indian instrument, similar to the Western oboe

simple time signature a time signature where the beat can be divided into two, such as 2/4 i.e. two crotchet beats, each made up of two quavers

solo a part for one instrument

sound modules devices that convert MIDI information into audio that can be played through loudspeakers

staff/stave the five parallel lines upon which music notation is written

stereo field the sense of space simulated by reproducing sound through two independent loudspeakers positioned to the left and right of the listener

subdominant the fourth degree of the scale

submediant the sixth degree of a scale

supertonic the second degree of the scale

syncopations notes accented off the beat. The weak part of the beat is often emphasised

tala the chosen rhythmic cycle of beats in Indian music played on the tabla drums

tan in Indian music, refers to the rapid scalic flourishes on the sitar/sarod or sarangai

teental common 16 beat (4+4+4+4) rhythmic cycle in Indian raga

tempo speed of the music

tenor C clef used in conjunction with the bass clef for high notes on the bassoon, trombone, cello, and double bass

ternary (ABA) a three part form. The first and last sections are identical or similar. The middle section (B) provides a contrast

tessitura the most commonly used part of the range of an instrument or voice

texture the number of parts in a piece of music and how they relate to one another. There are several distinct types. See **homophony, polyphony, monophony and heterphony**

theme and variations musical form featuring a theme followed by a set of variations on the theme

timbre particular tone colour of an instrument or voice

time signature the two numbers at the beginning of a piece of music. The top number refers to the number of beats per bar and the bottom figure indicates the type of beat, eg a 4= crotchet beats

tone interval of two semitones , eg F to G is made up of F to F# (a semitone) and F# to G (a semitone)

tone languages in African music, languages made up of only a few pitches, called tone languages. The pitch level determines the meaning of the words

tonic the first degree of a scale, the keynote ,eg. in c major the note c is the tonic note

treble (or G clef) this fixes the note G on the second line of the stave. The treble clef is used for high pitched instruments/voices

triad a three note chord ('tri' means three)

tutti means that everyone plays at this point in the music (Italian for 'all')

vaudeville a form of entertainment, popular in the 1700s, in which popular songs were performed with alternative words

velocities a piece of information included in a MIDI note which translates as the loudness of the note

verticalisation a method of producing chords in a serialist piece by playing adjacent notes of the series simultaneously

virginal small plucked string instrument like a spinet

virtual modelling synthesizer a software program which acts as a synthesiser, using the processing power of the host computer to copy aspects of another sound source and allow for manipulations of the sound that would not otherwise be physically possible

vocables effects made by the voice, using vowel sounds such as 'eh', 'ah', 'oh' etc

word painting describing words in musical terms. For example 'rising' would be set to a series of ascending notes or 'grief' by falling phrases etc

Index